Jürgen Franke
Gholamreza Nakhaeizadeh
Ingrid Renz
Editors

Text Mining

Theoretical Aspects and Applications

With 42 Figures
and 27 Tables

Physica-Verlag
A Springer-Verlag Company

Jürgen Franke
Prof. Dr. Gholamreza Nakhaeizadeh
Dr. Ingrid Renz
DaimlerChrysler AG
Research & Technology
Information Mining
Postfach 23 60
89013 Ulm
Germany
juergen.franke@daimlerchrysler.com
rheza.nakhaeizadeh@daimlerchrysler.com
ingrid.renz@daimlerchrysler.com

ISSN 1615-3871
ISBN 3-7908-0041-4 Physica-Verlag Heidelberg New York

Cataloging-in-Publication Data applied for
A catalog record for this book is available from the Library of Congress.
Bibliographic information published by Die Deutsche Bibliothek
Die Deutsche Bibliothek lists this publication in the Deutsche Nationalbibliografie; detailed bibliographic
data is available in the Internet at <http://dnb.ddb.de>.

Physica-Verlag Heidelberg New York
a member of BertelsmannSpringer Science+Business Media GmbH

http://www.springer.de

© Physica-Verlag Heidelberg 2003
Printed in Germany

Softcover Design: Erich Kirchner, Heidelberg

SPIN 10902493   88/3130/DK-5 4 3 2 1 0 – Printed on acid-free paper behavior demonstrated by users. Joachims also presents the results of different experiences in outperforming Google in terms of retrieval quality. His approach also seems promising for web usage and web structure optimization and personalization.

In their contribution "Towards Collaborative Information Retrieval", Armin Hust, Stefan Klink, Markus Junker, and Andreas Dengel report on the research results achieved at the German Research Institute for Artificial Intelligence in collaborative information retrieval (CIR). The main goal of CIR is to improve the accuracy of retrieval results by taking into account the interaction of different users with the retrieval engine. Furthermore, they illustrate CIR's relation to personalization issues, discuss some assumptions under which CIR can lead to better results, and argue that they are realistic and can be justified in many practical circumstances.

XDOC is a collection of tools organized in modules for the flexible and robust processing of documents in German, which was developed at Magdeburg University. Different XDOC features based on XML are described by Dietmar Rösner and Manuela Kunze in their contribution "The XDOC Document Suite - a Workbench for Document Mining". A number of techniques are implemented in XDOC to deal with lexical and conceptual gaps that are typical when starting a new application.

A typical burning issue in machine learning is the integration of available background knowledge in the learning process. Andreas Hotho, Alexander Maedche, Steffen Staab, and Valentin Zacharias address this issue in their paper "On Knowledgeable Unsupervised Text Mining" and discuss the importance of background knowledge for discovering meaningful relationships in a text collection. The authors introduce OSEM, which is an ontology-based framework allowing the integration of background knowledge.

At the end of the book, Fabio Ciravegna, Alexiei Dingli, Yorik Wilks, and Daniela Petrelli describe their ideas and the system realized for effective generation of annotated documents by "Using Adaptive Information Extraction for Effective Human-Centred Document Annotation". Two main problems have to be solved for such a system: timeliness and intrusiveness. The former shows the ability to react to new user annotations and the latter represents the degree to which the user feels bothered. Key ideas on solving these problems are presented and evaluated on a data set.

I would like to thank all the authors for their valuable contributions to the workshop and to the present volume, my colleagues in the Text Mining team of our department for their time and the effort they have spent on the organization of the workshop, and Reinhard Skuppin for supporting all organizational activities. And a special mention must be made here of Thilo Maier for his support in creating the layout of the manuscript. Thank you, everybody, this would not have been possible without your help.

Ulm, November 2002   *Gholamreza Nakhaeizadeh*

Foreword and Acknowledgements

This volume contains contributions presented at an international workshop held on April 26 and 27, 2002 at the DaimlerChrysler AG Research Center in Ulm, Germany. The main aim of the workshop was to discuss issues related to text mining and neighboring fields such as information retrieval and extraction.

In their introductory paper "Text Mining", Ingrid Renz and Jürgen Franke give an overview on the state of the art in text mining, focusing on applications at DaimlerChrysler Research.

XIRQL is an XML query language which enables records to be ranked based on specific parameters, e.g. uncertainty weights. Various features of XIRQL are described in the section contributed by Norbert Fuhr, "XML Information Retrieval and Information Extraction". The author also illustrates XIRQL's combination with information extraction. When information extraction is used for automatic XML markup of plain texts, XIRQL is able to consider uncertainty weights resulting from this process, and the markup leads to increased precision of text searches.

A wide variety of the problems arising in text mining are classification tasks. Aside from the different alternative approaches based on machine learning and statistics that can handle these tasks, a further viable method is the memory-based approach. In their paper "Feature-Rich Memory-Based Classification for Shallow NLP and Information Extraction", Jakub Zavrel and Walter Daelemans discuss the interesting aspects of this approach and illustrate its application to different text mining fields such as question answering and information extraction.

In their contribution "Concept Drift and the Importance of Examples", Ralf Klinkenberg and Stefan Rüping report on the recent results achieved in concept drift, which is, for the most part, a key controversy in machine learning and in information filtering (IF) in particular. In IF both the content of the documents used for learning and the interest of user may change over time. Therefore, systems that are able to capture such dynamic aspects can significantly improve the learning results. The authors address the role of examples in such systems and use an approach based on support vector machines to design a model that takes into account the different factors which can have an significant impact on the importance of the examples.

Design of functions to consider the users' preferences in ranking documents according to their relevance for a given query is the goal of the paper "Evaluating Retrieval Performance Using Clickthrough Data" by Thorsten Joachims. He introduces an SVM-based approach geared to automatically learn such ranking functions. He illustrates that the preference data needed is available in WWW search engines and can be inferred from the clicking

Contents

**Using Adaptive Information Extraction for Effective
Human-Centred Document Annotation** 153
Fabio Ciravegna, Alexiei Dingli, Yorick Wilks, and Daniela Petrelli

Text Mining

Ingrid Renz and Jürgen Franke

DaimlerChrysler Research & Technology, RIC/AM
D-89081 Ulm, Germany
{ingrid.renz, juergen.franke}@daimlerchrysler.com

Abstract. Text mining is a branch of data mining. Its objective is to analyze the texts of a complete text collection in order to select relevant texts or extracts, to categorize texts, and to give overviews of the text collection according to the user's interest. DaimlerChrysler research concentrates developing efficient and robust techniques from different disciplines (linguistics, in particular computational and statistical linguistics, information retrieval, and pattern recognition) for innovative text mining applications.

1 Introduction

Text mining can be defined as a special form of data mining (or knowledge discovery in databases) which is applied to large volumes of non-structured text files instead of to numerical, structured data. Thus text mining targets discovering and extracting knowledge from text documents.

The fastest-growing text database is the Internet, i.e. the World Wide Web. Yet in every organization, institution, company or even on any local computer, too, the amount of text is rocketing. Every scientist is familiar with the problem of the flood of papers that have to be read; every manager needs special information that can only be found by digging in large documents. For this reason, text mining is becoming more and more important to enable users to turn volumes of electronic texts into new information which is valuable for a variety of purposes.

The objective of text mining is to analyze a text or an entire text collection. Different results can be distinguished: texts from the collection are selected according to the user's interest, extracts taken from a text may be given or overviews of the texts presented. An extract is a helpful response when answering questions. A question-answering system analyzes a user's question and returns a sentence or text paragraph. Also, when a knowledge database has to be filled with information (e.g. facts taken from a newspaper or about a competitor), the filling of well-defined templates with parts of the analyzed text is an extraction task. On the other hand, overviews are given when information about a text is presented, e.g. collected summaries of one or more texts constitute an overview. Other overview tasks are providing information on which class a given text belongs to (categorization) or splitting a text collection up into undefined topics (clustering).

Mining techniques for analysis of single texts and large text collections differ significantly from those designed for analysis of structured data. The underlying reason is that texts are syntactically and semantically made up of meaningful words. In unrestricted domains, neither the meaning of single words nor the construction of context can be handled sufficiently well algorithmically. The complexity of human language, which is useful for communication, complicates any automatic analysis by computers. Nevertheless, for some well-defined tasks, different approaches to intelligent text processing have been developed in linguistics and information retrieval over the last few decades. Nowadays, these approaches are also used for text mining tasks.

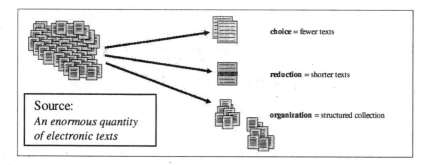

Fig. 1. Text mining objectives.

2   Text Mining: State of the Art

Text mining can hardly be characterized by its techniques since it merely borrows them from other disciplines such as linguistics or information retrieval. Instead of methods, applications are the common links between text mining activities. For this reason, we start with a short overview of related disciplines which influence text mining. Then, we address applications which are typical for text mining.

Traditionally, linguistics is the science which handles all the aspects of human language (including text): its origin, history, structure, usage. Since linguistics has a much broader interest in language, only special disciplines contribute to text mining. These sub-sciences examine individual issues relating to language, e.g. statistical characteristics of language, discourse elements in text, structural properties of sentences or phrases, or morphological construction of words.

2.1   Computational Linguistics

Computational linguistics is a research field between linguistics and computer science and focuses on the computational aspects of human language.

According to the subdivisions of linguistics, computational linguistics also examines the phonetic, morphological, syntactic, semantic and pragmatic facets of language.

There are theoretical as well as applied sides to computational linguistics. The objective of the theoretical direction is to gain new insights into human language ability. Language engineering, on the other hand, belongs to the applied side of computational linguistics. Here, the goal is to create systems that model or simulate parts of human language ability. Although state-of-the-art computational linguistics systems do not achieve overall human language ability, they can be integrated in various applications for human-machine interaction.

Computational linguistics is strongly influenced by techniques and methods of artificial intelligence. Hence, many systems are based on algorithms which use knowledge-intensive representations. These approaches are difficult to set up, maintain, or transfer to other domains. However, in well-defined applications, the benefits may be greater than the effort required.

When tackling text mining tasks, morphological analyzers and part-of-speech taggers are robust, fast, easy to handle, and useful elements of a system. A further technique for linguistic analysis that can be applied to perform text mining is information extraction.

Information Extraction. Information extraction is a research field which uses the results of computational linguistics and applies them to small, well-defined applications. When starting analysis of a text, the information to be found is defined by the user's interest (e.g. items in a template) and can be modeled by rules. Items of interest may, for example, be the names of companies or persons, facts and figures or more complicated events. The modeling must observe the linguistic variety typical for expressing meaning and has to be robust and fast if the system is to be useful (i.e. news reader).

In contrast to computational linguistics, it is not human language ability as a whole which has to be modeled, but only the ability that is used in a special domain. In this case, even more expensive methods can be efficient for analyzing real-world texts.

The main obstacle in integrating information extraction tools into text mining systems is the knowledge which has to be modeled for each domain and language. Current approaches towards combining machine learning and information extraction have to be carefully scrutinized.

2.2 Statistical Linguistics

Statistical linguistics has a long, unfortunately interrupted tradition. Today, the trend is to apply quantitative mathematical methods to all aspects of language and to all levels of linguistic analysis. But this was not always the case.

The theoretical foundation is that any text can be regarded as a result of stochastic, dynamic, non-recursive, non-stationary, and open processes.

Compared with computational linguistics, the chief advantage of statistical methods is that less external knowledge - which requires expensive maintenance - is necessary. But in order to find significant statistical rules, a gigantic quantity of text has to be analyzed. Depending on the linguistic level, anywhere from only a few megabytes are needed for the analysis of smaller linguistic units (for example, morphological analysis of words) to up to some gigabytes of text for semantic or pragmatic investigations of entire sentences, paragraphs or texts.

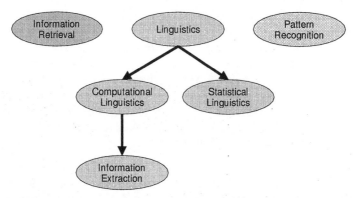

Fig. 2. Scientific disciplines which influence text mining.

2.3 Information Retrieval

Independent of research in linguistics, information retrieval has developed techniques which are particularly useful in text mining.

The primary objective of information retrieval is to search texts in a collection on the basis of a user's query. *"An intelligent retrieval system is a system with a knowledge base and inferential capabilities that can be used to establish connections between a request and a set of documents."* (Karen Spark-Jones). The set of documents is usually very large (giga- or tera-bytes of texts), whereas the request is a short statement (average length is 1.8 words). For this reason a third component is needed to transform documents and queries into a common language, which is the foundation of the retrieval system.

Most of the techniques of information retrieval can be applied to other text mining tasks such as categorization, filtering or clustering. The relationships between these disciplines are illustrated in figure 2.

2.4 Pattern Recognition

Independently of the above disciplines, the pattern recognition community has developed a variety of tools are suitable for application to text mining tasks. While some preprocessing of text documents is able to transform or represent the essential information of a text in a vector (see subsection 3.3, bag-of-words approach), there is no difference between tasks in text mining and pattern recognition: It is just analysis of sample sets in vector spaces.

Hence the techniques developed in pattern recognition can also be applied to text mining tasks:

- Feature reduction
  - Singular value decomposition
  - Principal component analysis
- Classification
  - Multilayer perceptron
  - Multireference classifiers
  - Support vector machine
  - Polynomial classifiers
- Cluster analysis

A key difference between pattern recognition and text mining applications is that the dimension of the feature space in text mining is often very large (some ten thousands) but very sparse (most of the features representing a text are zero). Another difference is that features often have a special relationship to each other resulting from their meaning. So, while in image understanding pixels typically do not have a special relationship to each other, a feature representing the word "car", for example, relates to a feature representing the word "automobile". But when these special relations are handled in preprocessing, standard pattern recognition techniques can be applied just as in common pattern recognition tasks.

2.5   Text Mining Applications

Since text mining is defined by its applications, we characterize some typical text mining tasks in this section.

Text Search. The most common text mining application is *searching texts* in a collection according to a user's query. If this query consists of single words or phrases, it is the classical information retrieval task. Every Internet surfer is familiar with this application and knows it as a "search engine" used to find web documents of interest. If the search is based not just on keywords, the application moves closer to text mining. Searches based on concepts use technology from artificial intelligence, searches based on overall text can profit from work in information extraction, and searches based on the preferences of other users are known as collaborative filtering. In any of these cases, a whole collection is analyzed in order to return one or more texts which correspond to the user's area of interest.

Information Extraction. Another noteworthy text mining application is the *extraction of information*. With respect to the pure number of texts retrieved in a search application, it is quite common that hundreds of texts (or even more) are returned to the user. In order to decide whether a specific text retrieved is relevant, an effective and short description of the text is essential. This description may be in the form of a few keywords which characterize the text, some concepts which are related to the text, a topic which the text belongs to or a summary of the text. In other applications, information extraction fulfills other tasks: it provides answers to questions or is used to fill a data base with facts from the texts. Here, the goal is to analyze a text - not a text collection - and to return relevant information about it.

Analysis of Text Collection. The third group of text mining applications aim at providing an *overview of a text collection*. Categorization and clustering tasks belong to this group. In categorization, classes (or categories) are given and the goal is to decide, for every text in the collection, which class it belongs to. Categorization is supervised learning, since for any class a number of examples exist as a training set and a classifier is trained in order to classify new texts. In contrast, clustering is unsupervised learning. Here, only texts of a collection without any class labels are used to group the texts together. From the perspective of the collection, both tasks split the overall collection into sub-collections. So, a collection is analyzed and this analysis returns groups of texts. But if we look at a single text belonging to the collection, the categorization result comprises information about the class, whereas the clustering result is solely which other texts are similar to it. These text mining applications can best be differentiated by answering two questions:

- What do they analyze?
- What is the result?

Table 1 is a matrix with these dimensions:

	analysis of single text	analysis of text collection
result is whole text	–	search, retrieval
result is internal information	key words, summaries	cluster
result is external information	class label, related text	categories, modified texts

Table 1. Characteristics of text mining applications

The first major characteristic of any text mining application is the distinction whether a text (which may be part of a collection) or an entire collection is to be analyzed. A text analysis may result in its keywords, in a summary or in a class label. A collection can be analyzed by splitting it into several groups which were either pre-defined (categorization) or built while computing (clustering). Every analysis of the collection also provides information about the single texts which constitute the collection, but the main interest lies on the collection itself. The second key characteristic is the result of the application desired. A search application returns a whole text. Further results which are directly text-based are single words (keywords) or text parts (used for summarization or answering questions). These results can be regarded as "text-internal" information. Text clusters are an internal result which is based on the collection itself. Another kind of result is external information: class labels in text categorization tasks, i.e. the information as to which category the text belongs. Or a bag of related texts, based only on similarity calculations, may be selected for any given text according to the texts' thematic contents and/or personalized profiles. Also, modified text in which the vocabulary is standardized or related to a taxonomy can be the result of a text mining application. This modification may have its origin in the collection itself (and is statistically computed) or in further knowledge bases (ontologies, taxonomies).

3   Selected Text Mining Projects at DaimlerChrysler

Work in text mining started at Daimler-Benz in the 90s with initial approaches to extracting information from (paperbound) structured documents. In order to enlarge the application focus, unstructured text was subsequently investigated. Here, the need to restrict the text domain has led to a burning issue: filtering or classifying text efficiently. Following the conventional pattern recognition experience at DaimlerChrysler Research, a tool box which was originally developed for information filtering from text has become the basis for our current text mining projects.

3.1   Information Extraction from Structured and Unstructured Documents

Structured documents are characterized by a well-defined layout, a rather formal structure (syntax), and a limited set of lexical entities within the text. The objective of information extraction from structured text is the extraction and interpretation of such structures. The results are entries which are inserted into a pre-defined template.

In order to extract the information captured by such structures, the system must have an explicit model (a kind of grammar) of the entities to be interpreted together with an interpreter. Thus, not only may typical techniques of artificial intelligence be applied, but also well-known compiler techniques. The representation language for modeling entities of structured documents is a semantic net language.

For the exemplary analysis of business letters (see figure 3), four structural entities have to be found and interpreted: recipient and sender, date, and

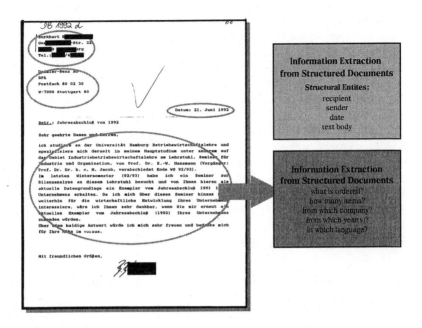

Fig. 3. Extraction task: analysis of business letters.

body of the text. In this application, two attributes are sufficient to extract objects from the pre-processed object set: box and content. They describe layout and lexical features, respectively. The recognition accuracy depends on the text quality and on the precision of the properties of the concepts to be interpreted.

The text body of a business letter usually consists of unstructured text, i.e. whole sentences. Again, the result of information extraction is a template consisting of different slots which are filled with concepts or facts from the text. This task can only be accomplished if the domain is suitably restricted. Looking at business letters, special inquiries for company's reports can be automatically analyzed and result in the extracted facts: kind of report (annual, long, thumbnail), origin of report (company), number of reports, language of report.

Our system for extraction from unstructured text consists of two parts. The first component is a general, domain-independent syntactic parser which transforms sentences into a list of semantic items in accordance with declarative linguistic knowledge bases (which are domain-dependent). The second part is a domain-independent template filler which transforms the resulting semantic items into template structures. Here, the knowledge models only the most common linguistic expressions in business letters.

For a well-defined sub-class of business letters (inquiries about reports), a complete system was developed and successfully tested. Since we carefully modeled the most typical linguistic expressions, the error rate is below 5% (assuming a rejection rate of about 20%). As to the efficiency of the components, all results are returned in less than 1 seconds, independent of input length.

3.2   Text Categorizer

Text categorization assigns pre-defined categories to the texts in a collection. This application is related to information filtering and message routing, which distributes text (for instance, news articles or mail messages, see figure 4) to specific people depending on the text category.

Typically, a text category is content-based, i.e. text categories represent different topics which depend on the current application. If newspaper articles have to be categorized, common topics are politics, the economy, sports, etc. If scientific papers are classified, the disciplines are the relevant classes. Topics in language identification are slightly different: texts are not distinguished by their content but by the language they are written in (e.g. English, German, Dutch).

Since we regard text categorization as a task of statistical pattern classification, two phases are distinguished. In an adaptation (or training) phase, labeled text samples are observed in order to learn features and classification rules. In the application phase, these features and rules are applied and new text objects are mapped into their appropriate categories.

First, our text categorization system transforms text into significant features. Then, based on these features, a message type is inferred. Features are computed from the training texts without external knowledge and are employed for text representation according to the vector space model. The vector space model is a representation of texts, which are converted into vectors. The features of these vectors are usually (selected) words in the text. The vectors are weighted to give emphasis to those that exemplify meaning and are useful for categorization.

Next, statistical classification techniques are employed for the inference, calculating the membership of every text vector. Those that are nearest to a class representative vector are considered to belong to this class. The dimensionality of the vector space can be reduced by linear transformation of the coordinate system, keeping the essential information. The classification principle is functional approximation based on polynomials. Another classifier which gives good categorization results in our applications is the single reference classifier. Every processing step uses knowledge which is adapted by statistical observations.

10   Renz, Franke

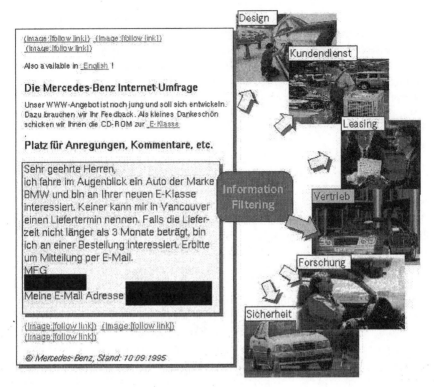

Fig. 4. Categorization task: distributing e-mails.

The key benefit of this approach to text categorization is the way the system is designed: it is a generic system which can be built automatically in very short time (few hours) once the training data has been labeled. Time-consuming manual construction of background knowledge and classification rules are avoided and the system can easily be adapted to new domains and different languages.

In 1997, we successfully took part in TREC-6, an international text retrieval conference organized by NIST (National Institute of Standards and Technology) where different approaches for information retrieval, routing (i.e. categorization), filtering, query answering, etc. are evaluated.

3.3 Search in Electronic Text Collections - Weaving Intranet Relations

Current projects which target retrieval of relevant texts from huge collections lie at the heart of the project "Weaving Intranet Relations" (WIR), which extends preceding knowledge management projects.

The challenge of WIR is to restructure intranets (and other web-based document collections) automatically. Here, restructuring means suggesting new hyperlinks between intranet documents. The outcome is an innovative tool which can be used in new applications in knowledge management, intranet technology or document management.

Each and every text in a given text collection is analyzed with respect to its similarity to other texts. This analysis yields suggestions as to where a hyperlink relation between texts would be sensible. All these automatically computed new hyperlinks are collected in a similarity matrix. Now, when intranet users read a text, they can ask for related texts and a collection of new hyperlinks from the matrix is presented. Also, for every new text, its similarity to all the other texts is computed, leading to a list of suggested hyperlinks. This feature is employed to retrieve information in response to a query - which can also be treated as text and similar texts searched for. Basically Weaving Intranet Relations offers an innovative retrieval function for an intranet. In addition, it is able to support organization and maintenance of the intranet content by proposing new structures and links.

The underlying technology in WIR is the computation of thematically-based text similarities. These texts may be linked in various ways (multidimensionality). WIR integrates algorithms of statistical linguistics, information retrieval, and statistical pattern recognition to compute the similarity of texts in a given electronic text collection such as an intranet. The main notion of our approach is that external knowledge (lexicons, terminology, concepts, etc.) is not used. Instead, exclusively collection-internal knowledge (i.e. statistics) is exploited. The system automatically adapts to any collection. For this reason, the technology can be used for texts in any language and on any subject.

The WIR system architecture is divided into an off-line computation which calculates the text relations and an on-line inspection of these relations given an query (i.e. in our system, an entire text).

The first procedure, the *calculation of similarities*, see figure 5, has to be done off-line, because it is time consuming. The entirety of the documents on the intranet are analyzed to capture the similarities of pairs of documents.

Calculating the similarities works as follows: A *text normalization* module converts the different formats of the real-world documents into a standard format (in intranet we usually find html files or documents from text processing applications; if this is not the case, the documents consist of plain text files which may contain special characters). *Texel generation* collects and counts all the texels (TEXt ELements, as per a pixel - picture element) in all the documents and the current ones for each document. Texels may be word forms, word stems or n-grams (letter strings of a given length) or even word combinations. *Feature definition* ascertains the best or most useful texels, defines them as *features*, and stores them in the *feature lexicon* for further analysis. This step substantially reduces the number of items: for example, in our intranet application with 60,000 documents comprising more than 200,000 words, this was cut to less than 20,000 features. *Vector generation* builds a feature vector for each document. On the basis of these feature vectors, the *similarity calculator* computes the similarities between documents as the distance between their vector representations. All similarities (above a given threshold) and other information about any text (keywords, summary, existing links, etc.) are stored and utilized for the second procedure: on-line presentation if similarities for a document are requested.

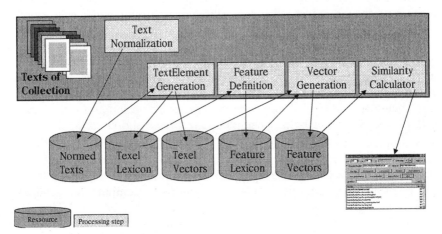

Fig. 5. Off-line calculation of similarities.

The second procedure, *requesting similarities* for a document, see figure 6, works on-line and is very fast. Given a document in the analyzed intranet, all similar documents listed in the similarity matrix are presented to the user. Since every web-surfer is familiar with a browser of some sort (Netscape Navigator, Internet Explorer), we employ this kind of software as output medium and show links to the closest documents, i.e. those documents with the greatest similarity to the source text.

For an intranet comprising 60,000 documents, off-line computation of the similarity matrix runs approximately two hours every night. Presentation of thematically-related documents takes less than a second. Presentation is triggered by a button "What's Related?", which is part of the browser's window and initiates the search in the similarity matrix. Figure 6 depicts the presentation of the "What's Related?" result.

The first version of the system was released to a major German company in October 1999. Further monitoring and feedback processes were implemented during the migration: monitoring makes the system robust and easy to use in everyday use, whereas feedback offers the only true evaluation, i.e. the welcome opinions of thousands of intranet users.

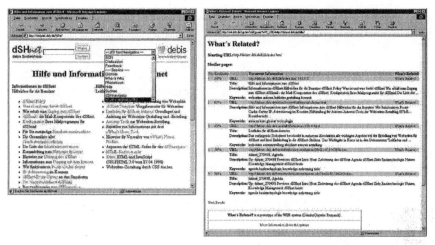

Fig. 6. On-line request of similarities and presentation of results.

When the WIR system returns a result, the user has to decide whether a proposed text is interesting solely on the basis of information about the path and filename of the text and a few keywords. In order to make this decision easier, we incorporated more (and better) keywords as well as short text summaries into the current release.

Keywords and summaries provide an overview of the text they characterize. Since we regard any text as a part of the collection if it is related to other texts, the computation of keywords also depends on these related texts. This results in adaptive keywords: in different collections, the same text is described by other keywords and summaries. Another way to enhance the overview of a document is to personalize keywords and summaries: previous user actions are examined and used as examples of the user's information needs (i.e. which documents has the user previously called). In any case, good keywords and summaries are essential to help the user get the relevant information quickly.

In a spin-off project "Looking for Others" (loofo), this analysis of an intranet is utilized to examine well-defined parts of the Internet. Although continually reading all the documents contained on a competitor's or partner's web server is a tedious task, it is vital for commercial organizations in today's highly competitive markets. Our technology supports this task by choosing the most relevant texts for which significant and characteristic information is extracted according to the specific needs of a user.

The same technology selects news articles (from accessible Internet and intranet sources) according to user profiles and builds a proposal for user-specific adaptive information. This information is then offered by an Info-Broker to a car's driver as infotainment. Previously read articles (together with any user feedback given) are stored in order to re-sort new articles, resulting in a more user-friendly ranking.

3.4   Analysis of Text Collections - Customer Feedback, Repair Descriptions, Accident Reports

Based on technology developed for analyzing web documents, a toolbox which offers text mining algorithms (preprocessing, outlier detection, clustering, categorization, duplicate detection, evaluation) was implemented. This toolbox is deployed in several projects where text collections from various sources and with different intentions have to be analyzed.

In business, often statements from customers about their satisfaction with a product or service or about their desires, needs, and problems have to be processed by employees. But how do we get an overview of the user's statements? Typically, an employee knows only the statements personally read. Even if a taxonomy for labeling is given, another employee might label the same statement differently. Moreover, errors in labeling are quite common. Even if a correct label is assigned to a statement, new and unexpected content would not be captured by a pre-assigned labeling. Another way to obtain new insights into an overall collection of customer feedback statements is the use of clustering techniques. Here, with similar techniques as deployed in WIR, various relationships between customer statements are identified. The entire collection can be divided into clusters of similar statements. This application finds unexpected information. If the clustering operation groups differently labeled statements into a single cluster, this indicates that these statements do not fit into the given labeling taxonomy. In this case, the taxonomy should probably be revised. Given all statements with the same label, the same technology is used to check the labeling. If the distance between some statements is greater than the mean, this indicates that these statements may be labeled incorrectly and should not be grouped with the other statements. Even if the only statements available are without any label, text mining technology provides new insights and content-based overviews. In particular, it finds clusters of interesting problems that would otherwise have been missed. Furthermore statement texts may be grouped according to topics without any human assistance.

Additionally, documents of various kinds play an important role in a user help desk: user queries, responses from employees, background information. Targeting improved service and reduced costs, text mining helps to facilitate the employees' work and to compose essential overviews of the current problem groups and tasks solved. Further applications making up this text mining toolbox are clustering of repair descriptions and categorization of traffic accidents reports.

3.5   Lemmatizing Vocabulary - Support for Help Desks

The variety that makes up human language is demonstrated in the different styles, different structures, and in different vocabularies. Various names are often used to denote a single entity (remember the example car = automobile). Although this characteristic of language enriches our communication, it can be a problem in some situations. One approach to handling variation in vocabulary is lemmatization, which groups different word forms together. These word forms may be similar with respect to form (i.e. art, artist, artistic) or content (i.e. jazz, music, saxophone). The dominant representative of each group is defined as the lemma, the other word forms are variants.

In a help desk environment, employees often have to cope with many different kinds of customers: laymen, users, specialists, other experts. These customers describe their problems in various ways. Also, the employee uses language in a specific way, i.e. jargon. And an expert, for example, may also communicate even more specifically. Lemmatization as a specific text mining technique helps to find related terms of users, employees, and experts by analyzing their texts. The automatic analysis splits the vocabulary into lemmata which variants are grouped to. This standardization does not restrict the vocabulary used by customers, employees, and specialists, but relates their different expressions instead.

This standardization of vocabulary is extremely promising. It can easily be integrated into the text mining applications previously mentioned as a new kind of feature reduction which preserves more information than the feature selection algorithms currently in use.

4   A Look Ahead

Since text mining at DaimlerChrysler is founded on statistical pattern recognition, it strongly prefers approaches which derive appropriate knowledge from texts of a given collection. For many applications, these approaches are efficient, robust, and successful. But there are text mining tasks, especially in information extraction, which require more external knowledge. Questions about which knowledge is needed, how it can be integrated into the existing approaches, and where it comes from will have to be addressed in the future.

Another characteristic of our current activities is that all text mining applications are thus far of a local nature. An interesting further step will be to employ our technology in (well-defined parts of) the Internet. This allows extraction of information from other people or organizations, usage of their knowledge, thus facilitating the work of information brokers whose job it is to observe what is going on.

Furthermore, it is foreseeable that new features will have to be integrated in text mining applications. Often, more than one language should be analyzed. So a key task will be to distinguish different languages and to mediate between them. In this are, translation - similar to linguistics - will be a much too complicated task, so that simpler approaches to bridging languages will have to be found. In addition to multi-linguality, personalization is essential feature for future text mining applications. The behavior of a user has to be monitored to be able to present more-relevant texts more flexibly. Since we can expect that the amount of text will continue to grow in our information- and knowledge-based society, there is clearly a need for techniques to tackle more and more text mining tasks. Thus, there remains a need for further research and innovative solutions.

Related Literature

1. James Allen. 1987. Natural Language Understanding. BenjaminCummings.
2. E. Charniak. 1993. Statistical Language Learning. MIT Press Cambridge.
3. Daniel Jurafsky, James H. Martin, Keith Vander Linden. 2000. Speech and Language Processing: An introduction to Natural Language Processing, Computational Linguistics and Speech Recognition. Prentice Hall.
4. Inderjeet Mani, Mark T. Maybury. (Eds.) 1999. Advances in Automatic Text Summarization. MIT Press.
5. Christopher Manning, Hinrich Schütze. 1999. Foundations of Statistical Natural Language Processing. MIT Press Massachusetts.
6. Maria Teresa Pazienza, J. Siekmann, J. G. Carbonell. (Eds.) 1997. Information Extraction: A Multidisciplinary Approach to an Emerging Information Technology: International Summer School, Scie-97, Frascati, Italy. Springer-Verlag.
7. C. J. van Rijsbergen. 1979. Information Retrieval. Butterworths Press London.
8. Gerald Salton, Michael McGrill. 1983. Introduction to Modern Information Retrieval. McGraw Hill.
9. Karen Sparck-Jones, Peter Willet. (Eds.) 1997. Readings in Information Retrieval. Morgan Kaufmann.

Department Publications

1. Thomas Bayer. 1993. Understanding Structured Text Documents by a Model Based Document Analysis System. In: Proceedings of International Conference on Document Analysis and Recognition (ICDAR-2). 448-453.
2. Thomas Bayer, Paul Heisterkamp, Klaus Mecklenburg, Peter Regel-Brietzmann, Ingrid Renz, Alfred Kaltenmeier, Ute Ehrlich. 1995. Natürliche Sprache - ein multimedialer Träger von Information InfoPort - ein Projekt zur Überbrückung von Medienbrüchen bei der Verarbeitung sprachlicher Information. In: G. Sagerer, S. Posch, F. Kummert. Mustererkennung 1995 (Proceedings of 17. DAGM-Symposium Mustererkennung, Bielefeld). Berlin: Springer Verlag. 428-439.
3. Ingrid Renz, Michael Stein. 1995. Domänenspezifische Deskriptorgenerierung zur Dokumentklassifikation. In: Tagungsband der 5. Fachtagung der Sektion Computerlinguistik (DGfS-CL'95), 4.-6.10.95, Düsseldorf. 84-89.
4. Michael Stein. 1995. Domänenspezifische Deskriptorengenerierung zur Dokumentklassifikation. Diplomarbeit. Fachbereich Informatik, Universität Kaiserslautern.

5. Thomas Bayer, Ingrid Renz, Michael Stein, Ulrich Kressel. 1996. Domain and Language Independent Feature Extraction for Statistical Text Categorization. In: Proceedings of AISB-Workshop Language Engineering for Document Analysis and Recognition, 2.4.96, Brighton.
6. Thomas Bayer, Ulrich Bohnacker, Ingrid Renz. 1997. Information Extraction From Paper Documents. In: P.S.P. Wang / H. Bunke (Hg.). Handbook on Optical Character Recognition and Document Image Analysis. Singapore: World Scientific. 653-678.
7. Thomas Bayer, Heike Mogg-Schneider. 1997. A Generic System for Processing Invoices. In: Proceedings of International Conference on Document Analysis and Recognition (ICDAR-4), Ulm, Germany. 740-744.
8. Thomas Bayer, Ulrich Kressel, Heike Mogg-Schneider, Ingrid Renz. 1998. Categorizing Paper Documents - A Generic System for Domain and Language Independent Text Categorization. In: Journal of Computer Vision and Image Understanding 70:3. Special Issue on Document Image Understanding and Retrieval. 299-306.
9. Thomas Bayer, Heike Mogg-Schneider, Hartmut Schäfer, Ingrid Renz. 1998. Daimler Benz Research: System and Experiments. Routing and Filtering. In: Proceedings of the Sixth Text Retrieval Conference (TREC - 6), Gaithersburg. 329-346.
10. Ralf Klinkenberg. 1998. Maschinelle Lernverfahren zum adaptiven Informationsfiltern bei sich verändernden Konzepten. Diplomarbeit. Fachbereich Informatik, Universität Dortmund.
11. Ralf Klinkenberg, Ingrid Renz. 1998. Adaptive Information Filtering: Learning in the Presence of Concept Drifts. In: Proceedings of Workshop Learning for Text Categorization (International Conference on Machine Learning - ICML / National Conference of American Association for Artificial Intelligence - AAAI), University of Wisconsin-Madison, Madison, WI, USA, 27.7.98.
12. Ralf Klinkenberg, Ingrid Renz. 1998. Adaptive Information Filtering: Learning Drifting Concepts. In: Technischer Bericht des FB Informatik der TU Berlin - Treffen der GI-Fachgruppe 1.1.3 (FGML98), Berlin, 17-19.8.98.
13. Christoph Peylo. 1998. Integration von Kontextinformation bei der Dokumentklassifikation. Diplomarbeit. Fach Computerlinguistik und Künstliche Intelligenz, Universität Osnabrück.
14. René Schneider. 1998. Automatic Acquisition of Lexical Knowledge from Sparse and Noisy Data. In: Proceedings of European Conference on Machine Learning, Chemnitz, Germany.
15. René Schneider. 1998. Maschineller Erwerb lexikalischen Wissens aus kleinen und verrauschten Textkorpora. Dissertation. Utz Verlag. München.
16. Ulrich Bohnacker, Jürgen Franke, Heike Mogg-Schneider, Ingrid Renz, Georg Veltmann. 1999. Restructuring Intranets by Computing Text Similarity. In: P. Sandrini (Hg.): TKE'99 - Terminology and Knowledge Engineering (Proceedings of TKE'99). Wien: Termnet. 610-617.
17. Carsten Lanquillon. 1999. Information Filtering in Changing Domains. In: Proceedings of the IJCAI'99 Workshop on Machine Learning for Information Filtering, Stockholm, Sweden.
18. Carsten Lanquillon. 1999. Evaluating Performance Indicators for Adaptive Information Filtering. In: Proceedings of the International Computer Science Conference (ICSC'99): Internet Applications, Hong Kong. Lecture Notes in Computer Science. Springer-Verlag.

19. Carsten Lanquillon, Ingrid Renz. 1999. Adaptive Information Filtering: Detecting Changes in Text Streams. In: Proceedings of CIKM99 - International Conference on Information and Knowledge Management, Kansas City, MO, 2-6. November 99. 538-544.
20. Ingrid Renz, Jürgen Franke, Ulrich Bohnacker, René Schneider. 1999. Querverbindungen schaffen. Ein innovatives Retrievalwerkzeug für elektronische Dokumentkollektionen. Wissenschaftsmanagement. Zeitschrift für Innovation. 28-31.
21. Ulrich Bohnacker, Lars Dehning, Jürgen Franke, Ingrid Renz, René Schneider. 2000. Weaving Intranet Relations - Managing Web Content. In: RIAO2000: Content-Based Multimedia Information Access, Paris (France), April 12-14 2000. 1744-1751.
22. Andrea Ficzay. 2000. Zustandsorientierte und dynamische Schlüsselwörter und Textzusammenfassungen. Diplomarbeit. Fachb. Informatik, Universität Ulm.
23. Carsten Lanquillon. 2000. Partially Supervised Text Classification: Combining Labeled and Unlabeled Documents Using an EM-like Scheme. In: Proceedings of the Eleventh European Conference on Machine Learning (ECML-2000), Barcelona, Spain. Lecture Notes in Artificial Intelligence, Springer Verlag.
24. Carsten Lanquillon. 2000. Learning from Labeled and Unlabeled Documents: A Comparative Study on Semi-Supervised Text Classification. In: Proceedings of the Fourth European Conference on Principles and Practice of Knowledge Discovery in Databases (PKDD-2000), Lyon, France. Lecture Notes in Artificial Intelligence, Springer Verlag.
25. René Schneider, Ingrid Renz. 2000. The Relevance of Frequency Lists for Error Correction and Robust Lemmatization. In: JADT2000 - International Conference on the Statistical Analysis of Textual Data, Lausanne (Schweiz), 9.-11.3.2000. 43-50.
26. Andreas Schorr. 2000. Auffinden logisch zusammenhängender Dokumente in einer Dateikollektion. Diplomarbeit. Fachbereich Informatik, Universität Ulm.
27. Ulrich Bohnacker, Lars Dehning, Jürgen Franke, Ingrid Renz. 2001. Automatic Analysis of Customers' Feedback and Inquiries. In: ICEIS 01 - International Conference on Enterprise Information Systems, Setúbal (Portugal), 7.-10.7.01. 1162-1165.
28. Ulrich Bohnacker, Andreas Schorr. 2001. Finding Logically Connected Documents in a Large Collection of Files. In: IAWTIC 2001 - International Conference on Intelligent Agents, Web Technology and Internet Commerce, Las Vegas (USA), 9.-11.7.01.
29. Ulrich Bohnacker, Andreas Schorr. 2001. Determining Logical Document Sets in File Collections. In: WebNet 2001 - World Conference on the WWW and Internet, Orlando (USA), 23.-27.10.01.
30. Carsten Lanquillon. 2001. Enhancing Text Classification to Improve Information Filtering. Fakultät für Informatik, Otto-von-Guericke-Universität Magdeburg.
31. Markus Ackermann. 2002. Lemmatisierung und Term-Clustering-Methoden zur Merkmalsgewinnung im Text Mining. Diplomarbeit. Universität Ulm. Fakultät für Informatik.
32. Heike Bieler. 2002. Dokumentenübergreifende Textzusammenfassungen. Diplomarbeit. Universität Potsdam. Institut für Linguistik / Allgemeine Sprachwissenschaft.
33. Ulrich Bohnacker, Lars Dehning, Jürgen Franke, Ingrid Renz. 2002. Textual Analysis of Customer Statements for Quality Control and Help Desk Support.

In: Proceedings of IFCS - 8th International Conference of the International Federation of Classification Societies, Cracow (Poland), 16.-19.7.02. Springer Berlin.
34. Markus Junker, Stefan Agne, Armin Hust, Stefan Klink, Christoph Altenhofen, Jürgen Franke, Ingrid Renz, Bertin Klein. 2002. Text-Mining in Adaptive READ. KI-Themenheft: Text Mining. 2/2002. 30-33.
35. Holger Hitzler. 2002. Erstellung eines adaptiven Nachrichtenassistenten mittels Benutzerprofilen. Diplomarbeit. Informatik, Fachhochschule Ulm. Schürfen statt surfen. Die Strategie für effizientes Suchen und Sortieren. DaimlerChrysler High-TechReport. 1/2002. 36-37.

XML Information Retrieval and Information Extraction

Norbert Fuhr

University of Duisburg
Information Systems
Institute of Informatics and Interactive Systems
47048 Duisburg, Germany
fuhr@uni-duisburg.de

http://www.is.informatik.uni-duisburg.de

Abstract. We present a new query language for information retrieval in XML documents and discuss its combination with information extraction methods. XIRQL is an XML query language which implements IR-related features such as weighting and ranking, relevance-oriented search, datatypes with vague predicates, and structural relativism. For information extracted from texts, XIRQL can rank records based on uncertainty weights, and single conditions may be evaluated using vague predicates for fact retrieval. When IE is used for automatic XML markup of plain texts, XIRQL is able to consider uncertainty weights resulting from this process, and the markup leads to increased precision of text searches.

1 Introduction

In many applications, large volumes of full-text documents are available. However, often the systems managing these large volumes of data offer only poor retrieval capabilities. Thus, the knowledge contained in the documents can hardly be exploited.

Currently, there is a trend towards XML as standard document format. For content based searches in full-text documents, XML offers two major advantages:

1. Since XML represents the logical structure of a document in explicit form, the retrieval system can return appropriate logical units as answers to content-based queries.
2. Based on the markup of specific elements, high-precision searches can be performed that look for content occurring in specific elements (e.g. distinguishing between the sender and the addressee of a letter, finding the definition of a concept in a mathematics textbook).

Unfortunately, most XML query languages proposed so far do not provide mechanisms for performing content-based searches in XML documents. In the following section, we present the new query language XIRQL (XML IR query language) which implements several IR concepts for XML retrieval.

Even under the assumption that XML will become the standard document format, there is still the legacy problem of large volumes of plain text. In order to apply XML retrieval mechanisms to these texts, automatic markup methods can be applied. However, due to the uncertainty of this process, subsequent retrieval of the documents prepared this way also should take into account this uncertainty. Since vagueness and uncertainty are central concepts of XIRQL, this can be easily accomplished.

As an alternative method to automatic markup, information extraction aims at the extraction of facts and knowledge from texts, in order to represent this information in a standard record format. Again, no perfect solutions for this process are possible, so the resulting uncertainty should be considered when accessing these records.

In Section 4, we discuss the relationship between automatic markup and information extraction and we show how XIRQL can be applied to the results of these processes. Finally, we give an outlook on further work in this area.

2 XML Retrieval

In XML documents, text is enclosed in *start tags* and *end tags* for markup, and the *tag name* provides information on the kind of *content* enclosed. As an exception to this rule, #PCDATA elements (plain text) have no tags. Elements can be nested, like e.g. `<author> <first> John </first> <last> Smith </last> </author>`.

Elements can also be assigned attributes, which are given in the start tag, e.g. `<date format="ISO">2000-05-01</date>`; here the *attribute name* is format, and the *attribute value* is ISO.

An example XML document follows , which also illustrates the tree structure resulting from the nesting of elements. Figure 1 shows the corresponding document tree (the dashed boxes are explained in section 3.2).

```
<book class="H.3.3">
  <author>John Smith</author>  <title>XML Retrieval</title>
  <chapter>  <heading>Introduction</heading>
   This text explains all about XML and IR.
  </chapter>
  <chapter>  <heading>XML Query Language XQL</heading>
   <section>  <heading>Examples</heading>
   </section>
   <section>  <heading>Syntax</heading>
      Now we describe the XQL syntax.
   </section>
  </chapter>
</book>
```

All XML documents have to be *well-formed*, that is, the nesting of elements must be correct (`<a><b></a></b>` is forbidden). In addition, a *document type definition (DTD)* may be given, which specifies the syntax of a

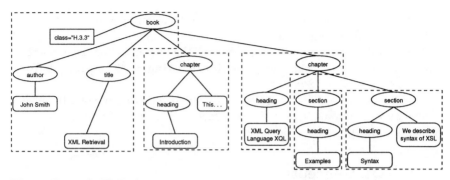

Fig. 1. Example XML document tree

set of XML documents. An XML document is *valid* if it conforms to the corresponding DTD.

XIRQL is based on the XPath standard [Clark & DeRose, 99], which was derived from the XML query language XQL [Robie et al., 98]; XPath also forms the path expression part of query language XQuery [Fernández et al., 01] proposed by the W3C. Here we give a brief description of those elements of XPath which are used in XIRQL.

XPath retrieves elements (i.e. subtrees) of the XML document fulfilling the specified condition. The query heading retrieves the four different heading elements from our example document. Attributes are specified with a preceding '@' (e.g. @class). Context can be considered by means of the child operator '/' between two element names, so e.g. section/heading retrieves only headings occurring as children of sections, whereas '//' denotes descendants (e.g. book//heading). Wildcards can be used for element names, as in chapter/*/heading. A '/' at the beginning of a query refers to the root node of documents (e.g. /book/title). The filter operator filters the set of nodes to its left. For example, //chapter[heading] retrieves all chapters which have a heading. (In contrast, //chapter/heading retrieves only the heading elements of these chapters.) Explicit reference to the context node is possible by means of the dot (.): //chapter[.//heading] searches for a chapter containing a heading element as descendant. Brackets are also used for subscripts indicating the position of children within an element, with separate counters for each element type; for example //chapter/section[2] refers to the second section in a chapter (which is the third child of the second chapter in our example document).

In order to pose restrictions on the content of elements and the value of attributes, comparisons can be formulated. For example, /book[author = "John Smith"] refers to the value of the element author, whereas the term /book[@class = "H.3.3"] compares an attribute value with the specified string. Besides strings, XPath also supports numbers and dates as data types, along with additional comparison operators like gt and lt (for > and <).

Subqueries can be combined by means of Boolean operators **and** and **or** or be negated by means of **not**.

For considering the sequence of elements, the operators **before** and **after** can be used, as in **//chapter[section/heading = "Examples" before section/heading = "Syntax"]**.

These features of XPath allow for flexible formulation of conditions wrt. to structure and content of XML documents. The result is always a set of elements from the original document(s).

3   XIRQL Concepts

3.1   Requirements

From an IR point of view, XPath lacks the following features in order to use it for content-based retrieval of XML documents:

Weighting: IR research has shown that document term weighting as well as query term weighting are necessary tools for effective retrieval in textual documents. These two types of weights should be considered during retrieval, thus resulting in a ranked list of elements.

Relevance-oriented search: The query language should also support traditional IR queries, whereby only the requested content is specified, but not the type of elements to be retrieved. In this case, the IR system should be able to retrieve the most relevant elements.

Data types and vague predicates: Since XML allows for a fine grained markup of elements, there should be the possibility to use special search predicates for different types of elements. For example, for an element containing person names, a similarity search for proper names should be offered. Thus, there should be the possibility to have elements of different data types, where each data type comes with a set of specific search predicates; these predicates also may be vague in the sense that they also may return weights between 0 and 1.

Structural relativism: XPath is closely tied to the XML syntax, but syntactically different XML constructs may express the same information. Thus, appropriate generalizations should be included in the query language.

In the following, we describe how these features have been integrated in XIRQL.

3.2   Weighting

Classical IR models have treated documents as atomic units, whereas XML suggests a tree-like view of documents. In order to develop weighting formulas for structured documents, we generalize the classical weighting formulas. The basic idea is to apply the classical weighting formulas to "atomic" units in XML documents. In addition, we need a combination rule for the case when larger units are retrieved.

We start from the observation that text is contained in the leaf nodes of the XML tree only. So these leaves would be an obvious choice as atomic units. However, this structure may be too fine-grained (e.g. markup of each item in an enumeration list, or markup of a single word in order to emphasize it). A more appropriate solution is based on the concept of *index objects* from the FERMI multimedia model [Chiaramella et al., 96] Given a hierarchic document structure, only nodes of specific types form the roots of index objects. In the case of XML, this means that we have to specify the names of the elements that are to be treated as index nodes. This definition can be part of the XML schema (see below).

From the weighting point of view, index objects should be disjoint, such that each term occurrence is considered only once. On the other hand, we should allow for the retrieval of results of different granularity: For very specific queries, a single paragraph may contain the right answer, whereas more general questions could be answered best by returning a whole chapter of a book. Thus, nesting of index objects should be possible. In order to combine these two views, we first start with the most specific index nodes. For the higher-level index objects comprising other index objects, only the text that is not contained within the other index objects is indexed. As an example, assume that we have defined section, chapter and book elements as index nodes in our example document; the corresponding disjoint text units are marked as dashed boxes in Figure 1.

So we have a method for computing term weights, and we can do a relevance based search. Now we have to solve the problem of combining weights and structural conditions. For the following examples, let us assume that there is a comparison predicate cw (contains word) which tests for word occurrence in an element. Now consider the query
//section[heading cw "syntax"]
and assume that this word does not only occur in the heading, but also multiple times within the same index node (i.e. section). Here we first have to decide about the interpretation of such a query: Is it a content-related condition, or does the user search for the occurrence of a specific string? In the latter case, in would be reasonable to view the filter part as a Boolean condition, for which only binary weights are possible. We offer this possibility by providing data types with a variety of predicates, where some of them are Boolean and others are vague (see below).

For the content-related interpretation, we think that the context should never be ignored in term weighting, even when structural conditions are specified; these conditions should only work as additional filters. So we take the term weight from the index node. Thus the index node determines the significance of a term in the context given by the node. For computing the weight of a term in an index node, we apply standard weighting schemes like e.g. tf·idf (treating index nodes like atomic documents).

With the term weights defined this way, we have also solved the problem of independence/identity of probabilistic events: Each term in each index node represents a unique probabilistic event, and all occurrences of a term within the same node refer to the same event (e.g. both occurrences of the word "syntax" in the last section of our example document represent the same event). Assuming unique node IDs, events can be identified by event keys that are pairs [node ID, term]. For retrieval, we assume that different events are independent. That is, different terms are independent of each other. Moreover, occurrences of the same term in different index nodes are also independent of each other. Following this idea, retrieval results correspond to Boolean combinations of probabilistic events which we call event expressions. For example, a search for sections dealing with the syntax of XPath could be specified as `//section[.//* cw "XQL" and .//* cw "syntax"]`. Here, our example document would yield the conjunction $[5, \mathrm{XQL}] \wedge [5, \mathrm{syntax}]$. In contrast, a query searching for this content in complete documents would have to consider the occurrence of the term "XQL" in two different index nodes, thus leading to the Boolean expression $([3, \mathrm{XQL}] \vee [5, \mathrm{XQL}]) \wedge [5, \mathrm{syntax}]$.

For dealing with these Boolean expressions, we adopt the idea of event keys and event expressions described in [Fuhr and Rölleke, 97], where we also show how correct probabilities can be computed for arbitrary event expressions.

In [Fuhr and Großjohann, 01], we describe how this approach can be easily extended in order to allow for query term weighting. Assume that the query for sections about XQL syntax would be reformulated as
`//section[0.6 · .//* cw "XQL" + 0.4 · .//* cw "syntax"]`.
For each of the conditions combined by the weighted sum operator, we introduce an additional event with a probability as specified in the query (the sum of these probabilities must not exceed 1). Let us assume that we identify these events as pairs of an ID referring to the weighted sum expression, and the corresponding term. Furthermore, the operator '·' is mapped onto the logical conjunction, and '+' onto disjunction. For the last section of our example document, this would result in the event expression $[q1, \mathrm{XQL}] \wedge [5, \mathrm{XQL}] \vee [q1, \mathrm{syntax}] \wedge [5, \mathrm{syntax}]$. In addition, we assume that different query conditions belonging to the same weighted sum expression are disjoint events and thus the final probability is computed as the scalar product of query and document term weights:

$$P([q1, \mathrm{XQL}]) \cdot P([5, \mathrm{XQL}]) + P([q1, \mathrm{syntax}]) \cdot P([5, \mathrm{syntax}]).$$

3.3   Relevance-Oriented Search

Above, we have described a method for combining weights and structural conditions. In contrast, relevance-based search omits any structural conditions; instead, we must be able to retrieve index objects at all levels. The index weights of the most specific index nodes are given directly. For the retrieval of the higher-level objects, we have to combine the weights of the different text units contained. For example, assume the following document structure, where we list the weighted terms instead of the original text:

```
<chapter> 0.3 XQL
  <section> 0.5 example </section>
  <section> 0.8 XQL 0.7 syntax </section>
</chapter>
```

A straightforward possibility would be the OR-combination of the different weights for a single term. However, searching for the term 'XQL' in this example would retrieve the whole chapter in the top rank, whereas the second section would be given a lower weight. It can be easily shown that this strategy always assigns the highest weight to the most general element. This result contradicts the structured document retrieval principle mentioned before. Thus, we adopt the concept of augmentation from [Fuhr et al., 98]. For this purpose, index term weights are downweighted (multiplied by an augmentation weight) when they are propagated upwards to the next index object. In our example, using an augmentation weight of 0.6, the retrieval weight of the chapter wrt. the query 'XQL' would be $0.3 + 0.6 \cdot 0.8 - 0.3 \cdot 0.6 \cdot 0.8 = 0.596$, thus ranking the section ahead of the chapter.

For similar reasons as above, we use event keys and expressions in order to implement a consistent weighting process (e.g. equivalent query expressions should result in the same weights for any given document). In [Fuhr et al., 98], augmentation weights (i.e. probabilistic events) are introduced by means of probabilistic rules. In our case, we can attach them to the root elements of index nodes. Denoting these events as index node number, the last retrieval example would result in the event expression $[1, XQL] \vee [3] \wedge [3, XQL]$.

3.4 Data Types and Vague Predicates

Given the possibility of fine-grained markup in XML documents, we would like to exploit this information in order to perform more specific searches. For the content of certain elements, structural conditions are not sufficient, since the standard text search methods are inappropriate. For example, in an arts encyclopedia, it would be possible to mark artist's names, locations or dates. Given this markup, one could imagine a query like "Give me information about an artist whose name is similar to Ulbrich and who worked around 1900 near Frankfort, Germany", which should also retrieve an article mentioning Ernst Olbrich's work in Darmstadt, Germany, in 1899. Thus, we need *vague predicates* for different kinds of data types (e.g. person names, locations, dates). Besides similarity (vague equality), additional datatype-specific comparison operators should be provided (e.g. 'near', $<$, $>$, or 'broader', 'narrower' and 'related' for terms from a classification or thesaurus). In order to

28   Fuhr

deal with vagueness, these predicates should return a weight as a result of the comparison between the query value and the value found in the document. The XML standard itself only distinguishes between three datatypes, namely text, integer and date. The XML Schema recommendation according to [Fallside, 2001] extends these types towards atomic types and constructors (tuple, set) that are typical for database systems. For this purpose, various type-checking mechanisms are provided, which operate at the syntactic level.

However, for IR applications, this notion of data types is of limited use. This is due to the fact that most of the data types relevant for IR can hardly be specified at the syntactic level (consider for instance names of a geographic locations, or English vs. French text). In the context of XIRQL, data types are characterized by their sets of vague predicates (such as phonetic similarity of names, English vs. French stemming). Thus, for supporting IR in XML documents, there should be a core set of appropriate datatypes and there should be a mechanism for adding application-specific datatypes.

As a framework for dealing with these problems, we adopt the concept of datatypes in IR from [Fuhr, 1999], where a datatype T is a pair consisting of a domain $|T|$ and a set of (vague comparison) predicates $P_T = \{c_1, \ldots, c_n\}$. Like in other type systems, IR data types should also be organized in a type hierarchy (e.g. Text – Western_Language – English), where the subtype restricts the domain and/or provides additional predicates (e.g. n-gram matching for general text, plus adjacency and truncation for western languages, plus stemming and noun phrase search for English). Through this mechanism, additional data types can be defined easily by refining the appropriate data type (e.g. introduce French as refinement of Western_Language)[1], by restricting the domain $|T|$ or by extending the set of vague predicates P_T.

In order to exploit these data types in retrieval, the data types of the XML elements have to be defined. For this purpose, we employ XML Schema, but use mainly the application info (which is treated like comments by the XML schema processor) for enumerating the vague predicates of a data type.

3.5   Structural Relativism

Since typical queries in IR are vague, the query language should also support vagueness in different forms. Besides relevance-based search as described above, relativism wrt. elements and attributes seems to be an important feature. The XPath distinction between attributes and elements may not be relevant for many users. In XIRQL, author searches an element, @author retrieves an attribute and ~author is used for abstracting from this distinction.

Another possible form of relativism is induced by the introduction of data types. For example, we may want to search for persons in documents,

---

[1] Please note that we make no additional assumptions about the internal structure of the text data type (and its subtypes), like representing text as set or list of words.

without specifying their role (e.g. author, editor, referenced author, subject of a biography) in these documents. Thus, we provide a mechanism for searching for certain data types, regardless of their position in the XML document tree. For example, #persname searches for all elements and attributes of the data type persname.

Further abstraction from the concrete XML syntax is possible by introducing datatypes. For example, a date value can be represented in various forms in an XML document, as illustrated by the following example:

```
<date year="2001" month="12" day="11"/>
<date>2001-12-11</date>
<date><year>2001</year>
    <month>12</month>
    <day>11</day></date>
```

With the 'date' datatype, users just specify the date in a standard format in their query and don't need to know how dates happen to be represented in the current document class.

4   XML Retrieval and Information Extraction

Information extraction (IE) deals with the problem of extracting facts and knowledge from texts ([Crespo et al., 02]). Typically, for a certain type of information need, a template is defined, which contains a number of slots (attributes, fields). Then the IE system processes text documents in order to extract the requested information; as output, instances of the predefined templates (records) are created, where the slots are filled with appropriate values from the text. Like in IR, this task is burdened with the intrinsic uncertainty and vagueness of natural language and its processing (e.g. in the examples in Figures 2–3, Raphael is recognized as a Baroque artist). Since the output of an IE system cannot be perfect, many systems assign uncertainty values to the instantiated templates. In addition, weights may be also attached to single fields of a record.

Instead of creating instantiated templates, the IE system also can be used for automatic markup (AM) of texts. In this case, values filling slots are marked up as XML elements with the corresponding element name. In addition, the whole text belonging to an instantiated template is marked up as an element; since there may be additional text not belonging to any of the slots, the template element has mixed content.

Table 1 compares IE with AM. IE presents facts out of context, but allows for surveys over a number of instantiated templates (e.g. in a table) and also enables post-processing of the extracted facts for text mining. In contrast, AM leaves the facts within the context, so the human reader can easily detect recognition errors and also take into account additional information from the text related to the template (e.g. the date '17th century' is modified in the

```
<Art> <Style> <Title>Baroque Art</Title> <Description> An arthistorical term
used both as an adjective and a noun to denote, principally, the style that origi-
nated in <Orig_Place>Rome</Orig_Place> at the beginning of the <Orig_Date>17th
century</Orig_Date>    superseding    <Related_Styles>Mannerism</Related_Styles>.
<Organisations>The Council of Trent <date>(1545-63)</date> </Organisations>
had strongly advocated pictorial clarity and narrative relevance in religious
art and to a degree Italian artists such as <Artist>Santi di Tito <date>(1536-
1603)</date></Artist> had responded with a more simplified style which
has been called <Related_Styles>'Anti-Mannerism'</Related_Styles>. Yet it
was not until the <date>17th century</date>, with the grounds well of re-
newed confidence and spiritual militancy in the <Organisations>Counter-
Reformation Catholic Church</Organisations> that a radical new style, the
<Related_Styles>Baroque</Related_Styles>, developed. Rome was the most important
centre of patronage at this period and the return to compositional clarity was
facilitated by a renewed interest in the antique and the <Related_Styles>High
Renaissance</Related_Styles> in the work of <Artist>Annibale Carracci</Artist>
and his Bolognese followers, <Artist>Domenichino</Artist>, <Artist>Guido</Artist>
<Artist>Reni</Artist> and <Artist>Guercino</Artist>. Their work is char-
acterized by a monumentality, balance and harmony deriving directly from
<Artist>Raphael<Artist>. </Description> <Source> </Style> </Art>
```

Fig. 2. Example text from an arts encyclopedia, with automatic markup.

```
[Template: Art_Style]
Origination_Place: Rome
Origination_Date: 17th century
Organisations: Council of Trent, Counter-Reformation Catholic Church
Artists: Santi di Tito, Annibale Carracci, Domenichino, Guido
Reni, Guercino, Raphael
Related_Styles: Mannerism, Anti-Mannerism, High Renaissance
```

Fig. 3. Extracted information from example

text to 'beginning of 17th century'). In addition, AM enables retrieval for
aspects not covered by the template, in combination with conditions referring to specific slots (for example, we could search for artists mentioned in
connection with the phrase 'religious art').

Information extraction	Automatic markup
facts out of context	facts in context
table-oriented view	document-oriented view
regular structure	irregular (text) structure
enables text mining	enables querying facts and (con)text

Table 1. Comparison of information extraction with automatic markup

For IE as well as for AM, the XML retrieval methods described above can
be applied. Since uncertainty is a central concept of XIRQL, the uncertainty
weights produced by the IE system can be considered during subsequent
retrieval.

- In the IE case, instantiated records can be represented as XML documents. Here XIRQL allows for ranking of records based on uncertainty weights produced by the IE system. In case the IE system has assigned weights to single elements, XIRQL would consider only those weights belonging to elements referred to in the query. Another potential benefit results from the concept of vague predicates in XIRQL, where records with values similar to those specified in the query also can be retrieved.

- AM does not only pinpoint the role of certain pieces of text, it also allows for the application of appropriate data types. Both features can be exploited in order to increase the quality of text retrieval: whereas the former serves as precision device, the latter may be used for increasing recall. Again, uncertainty weights produced by the AM system can be considered during retrieval. Query conditions may refer to marked up parts of the text as well as to the remaining parts.

The current version of XIRQL allows for the retrieval of complete elements of XML documents only. In contrast, XQuery supports the restructuring of results and also provides some aggregation operators. Both of these features are useful for text mining. However, a straightforward extension of XIRQL by these operators is rather difficult, due to the uncertainty weights that XIRQL assigns to the elements of the result.

As a simple example, assume that we have searched for documents dealing with XML retrieval, and — among others — we have found two papers by the author Smith, one with probability 0.6 and the other with probability of 0.7. Now we would like to know the number of papers each author has written on this topic, i.e. count the number of documents per author. For Smith, 3 answers are possible: With probability $0.12 = (1 - 0.6) \cdot (1 - 0.7)$ of his papers is on this subject, the probability of two papers is $0.42 = 0.6 \cdot 0.7$, and with probability 0.46, there is exactly one paper by Smith. So we would end up with a probability distribution instead of a single value. Alternatively, we could compute the expected value (which is 1.3), but this is still a floating point number and not an integer as in the deterministic case. So, both solutions yield results that do not conform to the type of answers in the deterministic case. Using expectations may be more attractive, but further processing of these values may lead to inconsistent results (e.g. the product of two expectations is not identical to the expectation of the product of the corresponding variables). So there is no theoretically satisfying solution to this problem. Instead a more pragmatic approach could be used; for example, one could use the top k answers from XIRQL and treat them as deterministic answers for the following processing steps, for which e.g. XQuery could be employed.

5   Conclusions

In this paper, we have described the requirements of IR in XML documents, and we have presented the query language XIRQL which fulfills these needs. For texts that are not available in XML format, information extraction and automatic markup methods can be applied. Whereas the former presents the information out of context and allows for further processing, the latter retains the context, thus enabling queries referring to both marked up facts and (con)text. In both cases, XIRQL is able to consider the uncertainty resulting from the preprocessing step. For text mining, further processing of the XIRQL results is necessary. Here appropriate methods for dealing with the uncertainty weights of the result elements still have to be developed.

References

[Chiaramella et al., 96] Chiaramella, Y.; Mulhem, P.; Fourel, F. (1996). *A Model for Multimedia Information Retrieval.* Technical report, FERMI ESPRIT BRA 8134, University of Glasgow. http://www.dcs.gla.ac.uk/fermi/tech_reports/reports/fermi96-4.ps.gz.

[Clark & DeRose, 99] Clark, J.; DeRose, S. (1999). *XML Path Language (XPath) Version 1.0.* http://www.w3.org/TR/xpath.

[Crespo et al., 02] Crespo, A.; Jannink, J.; Neuhold, E.; Rys, R.; Studer, R. (2002). *A Survey Of Semi-Automatic Extraction And Transformation.* http://www-db.stanford.edu/~crespo/publications/extract.ps.

[Fallside, 2001] Fallside, D. (2001). *XML Schema Part 0: Primer.* http://www.w3.org/TR/xmlschema-0/.

[Fernández et al., 01] Fernández, M.; Marsh, J.; Nagy, M. (2001). *XQuery 1.0 and XPath 2.0 Data Model.* http://www.w3.org/TR/query-datamodel/.

[Fuhr and Großjohann, 01] Fuhr, N.; Großjohann, K. (2001). XIRQL: A Query Language for Information Retrieval in XML Documents. In: Croft, W.; Harper, D.; Kraft, D.; Zobel, J. (eds.): *Proceedings of the 24th Annual International Conference on Research and development in Information Retrieval,* pages 172–180. ACM, New York.

[Fuhr and Rölleke, 97] Fuhr, N.; Rölleke, T. (1997). A Probabilistic Relational Algebra for the Integration of Information Retrieval and Database Systems. *ACM Transactions on Information Systems 14(1),* pages 32–66.

[Fuhr, 1999] Fuhr, N. (1999). Towards Data Abstraction in Networked Information Retrieval Systems. *Information Processing and Management 35(2),* pages 101–119.

[Fuhr et al., 98] Fuhr, N.; Gövert, N.; Rölleke, T. (1998). DOLORES: A System for Logic-Based Retrieval of Multimedia Objects. In: Croft et al. (ed.): *Proceedings of the 21st Annual International ACM SIGIR Conference on Research and Development in Information Retrieval,* pages 257–265. ACM, New York.

[Robie et al., 98] Robie, J.; Lapp, J.; Schach, D. (1998). XML Query Language (XQL). In: Marchiori, M. (ed.): *QL'98 — The Query Languages Workshop.* W3C. http://www.w3.org/TandS/QL/QL98/pp/xql.html.

Feature-Rich Memory-Based Classification for Shallow NLP and Information Extraction

Jakub Zavrel[1] and Walter Daelemans[2]

[1] Textkernel BV, Nieuwendammerkade 28/a17,
1022 AB, Amsterdam, The Netherlands
zavrel@textkernel.nl
[2] CNTS, University of Antwerp, Universiteitsplein 1, Building A,
B-2610 Antwerpen, Belgium
walter.daelemans@uia.ua.ac.be

Abstract. Memory-Based Learning (MBL) is based on the storage of all available training data, and similarity-based reasoning for handling new cases. By interpreting tasks such as POS tagging and shallow parsing as classification tasks, the advantages of MBL (implicit smoothing of sparse data, automatic integration and relevance weighting of information sources, handling exceptional data) contribute to state-of-the-art accuracy. However, Hidden Markov Models (HMM) typically achieve higher accuracy than MBL (and other Machine Learning approaches) for tasks such as POS tagging and chunking. In this paper, we investigate how the advantages of MBL, such as its potential to integrate various sources of information, come to play when we compare our approach to HMMs on two Information Extraction (IE) datasets: the well-known Seminar Announcement data set and a new German Curriculum Vitae data set.

1 Memory-Based Language Processing

Memory-Based Learning (MBL) is a supervised classification-based learning method. A vector of feature values (an instance) is associated with a class by a classifier that *lazily* extrapolates from the most similar set (*nearest neighbors*) selected from all stored training examples. This is in contrast to *eager* learning methods like decision tree learning [26], rule induction [9], or Inductive Logic Programming [7], which abstract a generalized structure from the training set beforehand (forgetting the examples themselves), and use that to derive a classification for a new instance.

In MBL, a distance metric on the feature space defines what are the nearest neighbors of an instance. Metrics with feature weights based on information-theory or other relevance statistics allow us to use rich representations of instances and their context, and to balance the influences of diverse information sources in computing distance.

Natural Language Processing (NLP) tasks typically concern the mapping of an input representation (e.g., a series of words) into an output representation (e.g., the POS tags corresponding to each word in the input). Most NLP tasks can therefore easily be interpreted as sequences of classification tasks: e.g., given a word and some representation of its context, decide what tag to assign to each word in its context. By creating a separate classification instance (a "moving window" approach) for each word and its context, shallow syntactic or semantic structures can be produced for whole sentences or texts. In this paper, we argue that more semantic and complex input-output mappings, such as Information Extraction , can also effectively be modeled by such a Memory-based classification-oriented framework, and that this approach has a number of very interesting advantages over rivalling methods, most notably that each classification decision can be made dependent on a very rich and diverse set of features.

The properties of MBL as a lazy, similarity-based learning method seem make a good fit to the properties of typical disambiguation problems in NLP:

- **Similar Input Representations Lead to Similar Output.** E.g., words occurring in a similar context in general have the same POS tag. Similarity-based reasoning is the core of MBL.
- **Many Sub-Generalizations and Exceptions.** By keeping in memory all training instances, exceptions included, an MBL approach can capture generalization from exceptional or low-frequency cases according to [12].
- **Need for Integration of Diverse Types of Information.** E.g., in Information Extraction, lexical features, spelling features, syntactic as well as phrasal context features, global text structure, and layout features can potentially be very relevant.
- **Automatic Smoothing in very Rich Event Spaces.** Supervised learning of NLP tasks regularly runs into problems of *sparse data*; not enough training data is available to extract reliable parameters for complex models. MBL incorporates an implicit robust form of smoothing by similarity [33].

In the remainder of this Section, we will show how a memory-, similarity-, and classification-based approach can be applied to shallow syntactic parsing, and can lead to state-of-the-art accuracy. Most of the tasks discussed here can also easily be modeled using Hidden Markov Models (HMM) , and often with surprising accuracy. We will discuss the strengths of the HMMs and draw a comparison between the classification-based MBL method and the sequence-optimizing HMM approach (Section 1.2).

1.1 Memory-Based Shallow Parsing

Shallow parsing is an important component of most text analysis systems in Text Mining applications such as information extraction, summary generation, and question answering. It includes discovering the main constituents of sentences (NPs, VPs, PPs) and their heads, and determining syntactic relationships like subject, object, adjunct relations between verbs and heads of other constituents. This is an important first step to understanding the who, what, when, and where of sentences in a text.

In our approach to memory-based shallow parsing, we carve up the syntactic analysis process into a number of classification tasks with input vectors representing a focus item and a dynamically selected surrounding context. These classification tasks can be segmentation tasks (e.g., decide whether a focus word or tag is the start or end of an NP) or disambiguation tasks (e.g., decide whether a chunk is the subject NP, the object NP or neither). Output of some memory-based modules is used as input by other memory-based modules (e.g., a tagger feeds a chunker and the latter feeds a syntactic relation assignment module). Similar ideas about cascading of processing steps have also been explored in other approaches to text analysis: e.g., finite state partial parsing [1,18], statistical decision tree parsing [23], and maximum entropy parsing [30]. The approach briefly described here is explained and evaluated in more detail in [10,11,6] [1].

Chunking. The phrase chunking task can be defined as a classification task by generalizing the approach of [28], who proposed to convert NP-chunking to tagging each word with **I** for a word inside an NP, **O** for outside an NP, and **B** for between two NPs). The decision on these so called IOB tags for a word can be made by looking at the Part-of-Speech tag and the identity of the focus word and its local context. For the more general task of chunking other non-recursive phrases, we simply extend the tag set with IOB tags for each type of phrase. To illustrate this encoding with the extended IOB tag set, we can tag the sentence:

```
But/CC [NP the/DT dollar/NN NP] [ADVP later/RB ADVP]
[VP rebounded/VBD VP] ,/, [VP finishing/VBG VP] [ADJP slightly/RB
higher/R ADJP] [Prep against/IN Prep] [NP the/DT yen/NNS NP]
[ADJP although/IN ADJP] [ADJP slightly/RB lower/JJR ADJP]
[Prep against/IN Prep] [NP the/DT mark/NN NP] ./.
```
as:

But/CC$_O$ the/DT$_{I-NP}$ dollar/NN$_{I-NP}$ later/RB$_{I-ADVP}$
rebounded/VBD$_{I-VP}$,/,$_O$ finishing/VBG$_{I-VP}$ slightly/RB$_{I-ADVP}$
higher/RBR$_{I-ADVP}$ against/IN$_{I-Prep}$ the/DT$_{I-NP}$ yen/NNS$_{I-NP}$
although/IN$_{I-ADJP}$ slightly/RB$_{B-ADJP}$ lower/JJR$_{I-ADJP}$
against/IN$_{I-Prep}$ the/DT$_{I-NP}$ mark/NN$_{I-NP}$ ./.$_O$

Table 1 (from [6]) shows the accuracy of this memory-based chunking approach when training and testing on Wall Street Journal material. We report Precision, Recall, and $F_{\beta=1}$ scores, a weighted harmonic mean of Recall and Precision ($F_\beta = \frac{(\beta^2+1)*P*R}{\beta^2*P+R)}$).

---

[1] An online demonstration of the Memory-Based Shallow Parser can be found at http://ilk.kub.nl .

type	precision	recall	$F_{\beta=1}$
NPchunks	92.5	92.2	92.3
VPchunks	91.9	91.7	91.8
ADJPchunks	68.4	65.0	66.7
ADVPchunks	78.0	77.9	77.9
Prepchunks	95.5	96.7	96.1
PPchunks	91.9	92.2	92.0
ADVFUNCs	78.0	69.5	73.5

Table 1. Results of chunking–labeling experiments. Reproduced from [6].

Grammatical Relation Finding. After POS tagging, phrase chunking and labeling, the last step of the shallow parsing consists of resolving the (types of) attachment between labeled phrases. This is done by using a classifier to assign a grammatical relation (GR) between pairs of words in a sentence. In our approach, one of these words is always a verb, since this yields the most important GRs. The other word (focus) is the head of the phrase which is annotated with this grammatical relation in the treebank (e.g., a noun as head of an NP).

An instance for such a pair of words is constructed by extracting a set of feature values from the sentence. The instance contains information about the verb and the focus: a feature for the word form and a feature for the POS of both. It also has similar features for the local context of the focus. Experiments on the training data suggest an optimal context width of two words to the left and one to the right. In addition to the lexical and the local context information, superficial information about clause structure was included: the distance from the verb to the focus, counted in words. A negative distance means that the focus is to the left of the verb. Other features contain the number of other verbs between the verb and the focus, and the number of intervening commas. These features were chosen by manual "feature engineering". Table 2 shows some of the feature-value instances corresponding to the following sentence (POS tags after the slash, chunks denoted with square and curly brackets, and adverbial functions after the dash):

[ADVP *Not*/RB *surprisingly*/RB ADVP] ,/, [NP *Peter*/NNP *Miller*/NNP NP] ,/, [NP *who*/WP NP]   [VP *organized*/VBD VP]   [NP *the*/DT *conference*/NN NP] {PP-LOC [Prep *in*/IN Prep] [NP *New*/NNP *York*/NNP NP]   PP-LOC} ,/, [VP *does*/VBZ *not*/RB *want*/VB *to*/TO *come*/VB VP] {PP-DIR   [Prep *to*/IN Prep] [NP *Paris*/NNP NP]   PP-DIR} [Prep *without*/IN Prep] [VP *bringing*/VBG VP] [NP *his*/PRP$ *wife*/NN NP].

Table 3 shows the results of the experiments. In the first row, only POS tag features are used. Other rows show the results when adding several types of chunk information as extra features. The more structure is added, the better

Struct.			Verb		Context -2			Context -1			Focus					Context +1			Class
			word	pos	word	pos	cat	word	pos	cat	pr	word	pos	cat	adv	word	pos	cat	
1	2	3	4	5	6	7	8	9	10	11	12	13	14	15	16	17	18	19	
-5	0	2	org.	vbd	-	-	-	-	-	-	-	surpris.	rb	advp	-	,	,	-	-
-3	0	1	org.	vbd	surpris.	rb	advp	,	,	-	-	Miller	nnp	np	-	,	,	-	-
-1	0	0	org.	vbd	Miller	nnp	np	,	,	-	-	who	wp	np	-	org.	vbd	vp	np-sbj
1	0	0	org.	vbd	who	wp	np	org.	vbd	vp	-	conf.	nn	np	-	York	nnp	pp	np
2	0	0	org.	vbd	org.	vbd	vp	conf.	nn	np	in	York	nnp	pp	loc	,	,	-	-

Table 2. The first five instances for the sentence in the text. Features 1–3 are the features for distance and intervening VPs and commas. Features 4 and 5 show the verb and its POS. Features 6–8, 9–11 and 17–19 describe the context words/chunks, Features 12–16 the focus chunk. Empty contexts are indicated by the "-" for all features.

the results: precision increases from 60.7% to 74.8%, recall from 41.3% to 67.9%. This in spite of the fact that the added information is not always correct, because it was predicted for the test material on the basis of the training material by the chunking classifiers.

Structure in input	Feat.	# Inst.	Δ	Prec	Rec	$F_{\beta=1}$	Subj. $F_{\beta=1}$	Obj. $F_{\beta=1}$	Loc. $F_{\beta=1}$	Temp. $F_{\beta=1}$
words & POS only	13	350091	6.1	60.7	41.3	**49.1**	52.8	49.4	34.0	38.4
+NP chunks	17	227995	4.2	65.9	55.7	60.4	64.1	75.6	37.9	42.1
+VP chunks	17	186364	4.5	72.1	62.9	67.2	78.6	75.6	40.8	46.8
+ADVP/ADJP chunks	17	185005	4.4	72.1	63.0	67.3	78.8	75.8	40.4	46.5
+Prep chunks	17	184455	4.4	72.5	64.3	68.2	81.2	75.7	40.4	47.1
+PP chunks	18	149341	3.6	73.6	65.6	69.3	81.6	80.3	40.6	48.3
+ADVFUNCs	19	149341	3.6	74.8	67.9	**71.2**	81.8	81.0	46.9	63.3

Table 3. Results of grammatical relation assignment with increasing levels of structure in the test data added by earlier modules in the cascade. Columns show the number of features in the instances, the number of instances constructed from the test input, the average distance between the verb and the focus element, precision, recall and $F_{\beta=1}$ over all relations, and $F_{\beta=1}$ over some selected relations (from [6]).

1.2 Hidden Markov Models

Except for the grammatical relation finder described in the previous section, all components of the memory-based shallow parser could also be modeled using Hidden Markov Models. An HMM is a finite state automaton with probabilities attached to state transitions and to symbol emissions [27]. The models are called 'Hidden' because we can not uniquely deduce which path the automaton took through its state space from the observation of an emitted symbol sequence. Tagging can be represented in an HMM by modeling tags as states, so that the transition probability $P(t_i|t_{i-1})$ corresponds to the conditional probability of seeing tag t_i after tag t_{i-1}. The emission probabilities $P(w_j|t_i)$ correspond to the chance of seeing a particular word w_j when being in state t_i. These probabilities can be estimated from relative frequencies in a tagged corpus, and are usually smoothed to accommodate for sparse data and supplemented with a separate unknown word 'guesser' module to provide lexical probabilities for out of vocabulary words. A sequence of symbols is tagged by finding the most probable path through the state space, given the model's parameters and the input sequence.

A tag bigram model can in some sense only look at the previous tag in the sequence and the lexical probabilities of the current word as an information source for disambiguation. Richer information sources (i.e., features) can be modeled by making the state space more complex, e.g., by having states for every pair of tags, as is the case in typical trigram POS taggers [8,14,4]. An HMM can also be interpreted as a sequence of classification decisions, namely each step through the model classifies the present word given the previous decision (or the previous two decisions in the case of trigram taggers) and the word itself (the features). However, in contrast to e.g. the memory-based classification models described above, HMMs do not commit to the previous decision and move on. The search for the most probable path takes each 'classification' at step $i - 1$ into account, together with its probability, so that all possible tag sequences are considered. In this way, a locally good classification (based on only two features 'word' and 'tag-1' can be overridden because it leads to a less likely path later in the sequence.

Due to this property, the HMM's information horizon can effectively be much larger that the explicit number of features it uses. In combination with effective smoothing and unknown word guessing techniques, and the fact that the small number of features allows for robust parameter estimation from even very modest amounts of training data, this makes a good implementation of a trigram HMM difficult to beat for POS tagging.

	LOB	WSJ	Wotan	WotanLite
Transformation-Based	96.37	96.28	–	94.63
Memory-Based	97.06	96.41	89.78	94.92
Maximum-Entropy	97.52	**96.88**	91.72	**95.56**
TnT	**97.55**	96.63	**92.06**	95.26

Table 4. The accuracy of feature-rich vs. HMM taggers on four POS datasets.

Table 4 shows how Trigrams 'n Tags (TnT) [4], rivals three other, feature-rich and classification-based algorithms [2] on a number of corpora.

---

[2] The Maximum Entropy-based tagger MXPOST [29], the Transformation-based tagger of [5], and the Memory-based tagger MBT [10] (adapted from [19]).

Many modern approaches to Information Extraction also make use of Hidden Markov Models or variants thereof [3,16,24]. An Information Extraction task is typically modelled with an HMM that has a background state (or empty tag) for all words except a phrase to be extracted and a filler state (or extract tag) for the phrase that is a filler for a field to be extracted. Several variations on this setup have shown to be surprisingly accurate in comparison to various rule-learning methods. There are however, two important issues with this straightforward use of HMMs in Information Extraction. First, the HMMs are fundamentally short-sighted to the larger lexical context. In semi-structured text, an instance of a filler string is often preceded by a quasi-regular context. E.g., in the seminar announcement data set discussed below, a speaker instance is often preceded by phrases like: "Who :", "featuring", or followed by phrases like "will give a talk", "will discuss", etc. An HMM with only states for background and filler tags will never be able to make use of such information: The typical left context of a phrase of interest will be generated from the background state, just as other irrelevant parts of the document. The transition from the background state to the filler state will not become more likely by the occurrence of the informative cue phrase. In the works cited above, this has been dealt with, either by modifying the standard conditioning of the state transition probability from $P(t_i|t_{i-1})$ to $P(t_i|t_{i-1}, w_{i-1})$ [3], or by modifying the state space of the HMM so that special *prefix* and *suffix* states are reserved to tag the left and right context of the filler [16,17]. These modifications have shown to work very well in experimental comparisons, making HMMs the state-of-the-art method for Information Extraction. A second problem in the HMM framework is how to use diverse information sources. In many interesting IE domains success may depend on knowledge of the syntactic structure, or on the paragraph, discourse, or layout structure of the whole text. It is possible to incorporate these types of information in the model's state space as well. However, the room for maneuvering is limited. Each additional feature that is factored into the state space increases its size multiplicatively. This leads to an exponential slowdown of the HMM, whose tagging speed is quadratic in the size of the state space, and to exponential increase of data sparsity. The effects of data sparsity can be mitigated by effective smoothing techniques, such as deleted interpolation, or shrinkage [16]. Shrinkage, for example, interpolates the probability distributions between complex states in a model and similar states in simpler versions of the model. However, the need to define an explicit back-off ordering from specific complex states to similar but more general states leads to a combinatorial explosion as well [33]. In contrast, Memory-Based Learning, and other classification-based frameworks, can provide better solutions for these complex modeling problems by factoring the fusion of information sources into the feature space rather than into the state space.

2   Memory-Based Information Extraction

The task of Information Extraction (IE), arguably the core activity in the field of text mining, is to extract specific pre-defined types of information from unrestricted text; i.e. finding fillers in a text for predefined slots in some template. In current approaches to IE using supervised machine learning, extraction patterns are learned on the basis of linguistically enriched corpora, and the patterns are, possibly after manual post-processing, used in IE systems [31,20,32,7].

However, it is also possible to interpret IE as a classification task, similar to NLP tasks like POS tagging and chunking. The input representation is a word and (information about) its context, and the output is either the background class *none*, or one of the slot filler classes. For example, in a hypothetical IE system for terrorist attacks, the following mapping can be learned as a supervised classification-based task.

John/I-victim Doe/I-victim , minister/*none* of/*none*
language/*none* technology/*none* was/*none* killed/*none* by/*none*
a/*none* car/I-weapon bomb/I-weapon yesterday/I-time
evening/I-time ./*none*

From this tagged sentence the following template could be extracted:

Victim:	John Doe
Weapon:	car bomb
Time:	yesterday evening

We can also choose to assign, in one or several steps of classification, much more structure to the input than just the phrases to be extracted. For example, the title and author information of this paper might be tagged with section information and shallow syntactic structure as follows:

```
Feature-Rich    JJ:NP[:I-title
Memory-Based    JJ:NP:I-title:I-topic
Classification  NN:NP]:I-title:I-topic
for IN:PP[:I-title
Information NN:PP[:NP[:I-title:I-topic
Extraction   NN:PP]:NP]:I-title:I-topic}
XXXBLANKXXX none
Jakub    NNP:NP[:I-authors:I-name
Zavrel   NNP:NP]:I-authors:I-name
and CC:I-authors
Walter   NNP:NP[:I-authors:I-name
Daelemans    NNP:NP]:I-authors:I-name
```

```
Textkernel   NNP:NP[:I-authors:I-organisation
BV   NNP:NP]:I-authors:I-organisation
,    ,:I-authors
Nieuwendammerkade   NNP:NP[:I-authors:I-address
28   a17 SYM:NP]:I-authors:I-address
,    ,:I-authors:I-address
1022   CD:NP[:I-authors:I-address
AB   NNP:NP]:I-authors:I-address
,    ,:I-authors:I-address
Amsterdam   NNP:NP[]:I-authors:I-address
,    ,:I-authors:I-address
The DT:NP[:I-authors:I-address
Netherlands NNP:NP]:I-authors:I-address
CNTS     SYM:NP[]:I-authors:I-organisation
,    ,:I-authors:I-organisation
University   NNP:NP[:I-authors:I-organisation
of   NNP:NP[:I-authors:I-organisation
Antwerp NNP:NP[:I-authors:I-organisation
,    ,:I-authors
Universiteitsplein   NNP:NP[:I-authors:I-address
1    CD:NP]:I-authors:I-address
,    ,:I-authors:I-address
Building     NN:NP[:I-authors:I-address
A    SYM:NP:I-authors:I-address
,    ,:I-authors:I-address
B-2610   SYM:NP[]:I-authors:I-address
Antwerpen    NNP:NP[]:I-authors:I-address
,    ,:I-authors:I-address
Belgium NNP:NP[]:I-authors:I-address
```

Leading to the following XML structure (leaving POS tags aside):

```
<title>
<np>Feature-Rich <topic>Memory-Based Classification</topic></np>
<pp>for <np><topic>Information Extraction</topic></np></pp>
</title>
<authors>
<name><np>Jakub Zavrel</np></name> and
<name><np>Walter Daelemans</np></name>
<organisation><np>Textkernel BV</np></organisation>,
<address><np>Nieuwendammerkade 28/a17</np>, <np>1022 AB</np>,
<np>Amsterdam</np>, <np>The Netherlands</np></address>
<organisation><np>CNTS</np>, <np>University of Antwerp</np>,
<address><np>Universiteitsplein 1</np>, <np>Building A</np>,
<np>B-2610</np> Antwerpen, Belgium</np></address>
</authors>
```

In an HMM approach, such codings will lead to an explosion of the state space, or a necessary decomposition of the task into a sequence of many small sub-problems. However, from an informational point of view, there are probably many interesting dependencies between decisions at various levels of structure. A feature-rich classification-based approach, such as Memory-Based Learning, allows a representation of such tasks as either monolithic classification tasks, or decomposed cascades or ensembles of tasks, whatever is best for accuracy and speed. When cascading Memory-Based classifiers, we can always train a higher level of classification to use the outputs of lower levels as input features.

2.1   TK_SemTagger

We have implemented a general environment called **TK_SemTagger** as part of Textkernel's Textractor toolkit in order to allow experimentation with the Memory-Based tagging approach to IE. In Textractor, we use this component side by side with HMMs, induced extraction rules and Shallow NLP preprocessing to benefit from the complementary strengths of all methods.

Architecture. During training, the tagger reads in the training corpus, and constructs a corpus based lexicon (see below). If needed it also reads in other information sources, such as a domain lexicon, and connects to external NLP pre-processors. Then the training corpus is converted into training instances (feature vectors) according to a flexible feature set specification. These instances are used to train a Memory-based classifier (TiMBL [13], an efficient implementation of MBL). The manner in which cases are retrieved from memory, the metric used for computing similarity, the way features are weighted, the number of nearest neighbors used, and the weighting of neighbors during extrapolation are all parameterized. For a full discussion of TiMBL's parameters we refer the reader to [13].

After training the classifier, test data is processed given the same feature set specification, and each token is classified. The test data is processed sentence by sentence (for the IE tasks described below, a 'sentence' is a whole document). Each sentence is processed from left to right, so that previous classification decisions are propagated to the left context (for use as features in subsequent decisions). TK_SemTagger also allows the use of an *ensemble* of classifiers (e.g., with different features or different parameters), which can have dependencies between each other. The ensembles are combined by stacking (two levels: L1 and L2). The classifiers in level L2 are applied *after* the L1 classifiers have tagged the entire sentence, and hence can refer to decisions made by L1 classifiers both to the left and the right of the word to be tagged. In the present study, however, no exploration was made of ensemble systems.

Lexical Information. Tagging is an exercise in the satisfaction of two simultaneous constraints: lexical possibilities of a word and contextual possibilities. In HMM-based taggers, the lexicon (or the unknown word guesser) typically proposes a selection of tags for the present word, and the tags that are most compatible with the present context are selected. In classification-based tagging, in contrast, the lexical representations of a word are seen as yet another symbolic feature. This gives us greater freedom, as we can also assign a tag that is not in a word's lexical representation (and it is well-known that lexicons are seldom complete). We can even use a lexicon that contains tags from a completely different tag set [34].

The most important lexical information in our Memory-Based IE approach is compiled directly from the training corpus. We record the number of times each word has been used with each tag. To convert this frequency information into a symbolic feature, the set of tags for a word is sorted by frequency, and the tags that fall below a percentage threshold are pruned away. An empirically derived good default value for this threshold is 5%. In addition to this, words that occur very often (more than 25 times) and have no ambiguous occurrences are labeled 'sure thing'. This means that during tagging, their lexical tag is assigned without looking at the context. Since the lexical ambiguity class of a word is just another feature, we are able to use any number of different lexicons, such as e.g. domain-specific ontologies or gazetteers. However, in the present experiments this option was not used.

Features. A case for classification can be represented using a multitude of features. The features are specified as a template of positions and types. The best setting depends on the task at hand, the selected features and their representation, the amount of data, and the used TiMBL parameters. The following types are available at each position i.

- **word**: gives the string of the word at position i.
- **wordf***expr*: where *expr* is a constraint on the frequency of the word to be included as a feature (e.g., 'wordf>5' or 'wordf<=10').
- **tag**: gives the full tag of the word at position i. This feature refers to a decision of the current classifier on an earlier word in the sentence, and can therefore only be used on positions in the left context.
- **known**: has a value of 'KNOWN' for words that have been seen in the training corpus, and a value of 'UNKNOWN' for words that did not occur in it.
- **lex**: gives the lexical representation (ambiguity class) of the word, as found in the lexicon constructed from the training corpus (see section 2.1).
- **domlex**: gives the lexical representation (ambiguity class) of the word as found in an externally supplied lexicon with domain knowledge.
- **exttag**: gives the tag given to a position by an external tagger, chunker or other syntactic pre-processor.

- **prev:***tag2*: this is a binary feature. It is on if *tag2* (a second level tag) is present somewhere in the left history of previous tagging decisions. I.e. this feature means 'have seen *tag2* before'. This type of feature can only be used for the position of the word that is to be tagged, not in left and right context positions.
- **suf***n*: a family of suffix features. 'suf*n* gives the *n*'th letter from the end of the word (e.g., 'suf1' of "bread" is "d", and 'suf3' is "e"). When *n* is given as a range, e.g., 'suf1-3', the value is the suffix between first and last number in the range (e.g., 'suf1-3' of "bread" is "ead").
- **pref***n*: a family of prefix features. Works analogously to 'suf'.
- **num**: a binary feature that indicates the presence of a numeric character in the word.
- **allnum**: a binary feature that indicates whether the token consist of numeric symbols, and possibly punctuation, only.
- **hyp**: a binary feature that indicates the presence of a hyphen in a word.
- **at**: a binary feature that indicates the presence of an 'at' sign ("") in a word.
- **und**: a binary feature that indicates the presence of an underscore in a word.
- **cap**: a binary feature that indicates the presence of a capital letter in a word.
- **allcap**: a binary feature that indicates whether the token is fully capitalized.
- **L1-***name*: a feature that refers to a decision of another classifier (named L1-*name*), that has been applied before the present one. When L1- *name* is the same as that of the current classifier, the result is the same as that of the 'tag' feature. This feature is used to define dependencies between classifiers in an ensemble. It was not used in the present experiments.

The feature template represents a window of word positions to the left (negative numbers) and to the right (positive numbers) of the focus word (the word to be tagged, i.e. position '0'). If any of the specified features refer to the output of another classifier, i.e. when a bootstrap dependency exists, this is solved by using features produced by cross-validating the other classifier on the training set. Figure 1 shows an example of a feature set for one classifier.

3   Data

We performed experiments comparing the TnT implementation of HMMs and the feature rich **TK_SemTagger** approach on two IE tasks. The first, the **Seminar Announcement** data set consists of 485 usenet postings concerning academic seminar announcements. The collection was collected and manually annotated by [15] [3] The set of documents is labeled with four fields

---

[3] Available from the RISE repository at
http://www.isi.edu/~muslea/RISE/repository.html.

```
classifier: L1-A
features:
-4 tag wordf>4
-3 tag wordf>4
-2 tag wordf>4
-1 tag wordf>4
0 wordf>4 lex suf1 suf2 pref1 initonlycap initial allcap cap hyp num at
1 lex wordf>4
2 lex wordf>4
3 lex wordf>4
4 lex wordf>4
parameters: -mM -k3 -w4 -dIL
```

Fig. 1. Example of a feature configuration (the best configuration on the Seminar Announcement data set). The Timbl parameters shown are: MVDM; Shared variance weighting; 3 nearest neighbors; Dudani distance weighted voting.

to be extracted: *speaker, location, stime* (start time), and *etime* (end time). In the original work on this dataset, a 'One Best per Document' (OBD) scoring method was used. This means that if the extraction method can fill an entity slot with any one of the occurrences of that entity in the text, this is counted as correct. However, in the data, all occurrences are marked. In our experiments we have taken a slightly more challenging scoring metric: *Each occurrence* of an entity must be labeled with exactly matching boundaries by the tagger. We used the first half of the data set for training, the first 40 documents from the second half for validation of parameters, and documents 40 through 80 from the second half for testing.

The second task we report results on is the task of populating a database from a set of CVs. The data is a set of 103 **German Curriculum Vitae** that were spidered from the web, and manually annotated with XML structure. Both section information (personal information, work experience, education, other), and extractable entity information was annotated. The following fields are to be extracted: *name address, phone, email, birthday, marstat* (marital status), *military* (military service), *compskill* (computer skills), *degree, degreedate, experience, experiencedate, langskill* (language skill), and *langprofi* (language proficiency). Since the data set is so small (although it leads to more than 50000 token classification cases), we used the first 10 documents for validation, and the rest for training during tuning, and we report ten-fold cross validation results over the whole dataset for comparing algorithms. Arguably, this puts the more tuned system, (Timbl has four parameters in this experiment, whereas TnT only has one) in a slightly more favorable position. For both datasets, we report $F_{\beta=1}$ scores.

4 Experiments

4.1 HMM Results

With the TnT HMM model we tested two variants. The first variant, TnT Simple, has a state for each filler type, and a background state for the re-

46   Zavrel, Daelemans

mainder of the text. The second variant, TnT Context, has a set of prefix and
suffix states, one of each for each type of filler, that is applied to respectively
two tokens before, and two tokens after the filler. As can be seen in Figures 5
and 6, the TnT Context model clearly outperforms the TnT Simple model
on average. Interestingly, this does not happen on the *email, langskill,* and
military fields of the German CV task, showing that for these fields the lexical content of the filler, rather than some cue phrases typically preceding or
following it, is a strong enough feature to accurately make the decision. The
TnT Context model suffers in these places from the additional data sparse-
ness introduced by the prefix and suffix states. Increasing the context size for
the prefix and suffix states did not further improve performance.

	speaker	location	stime	etime
TnT Context	**0.66**	**0.70**	**0.85**	**0.90**
TnT Simple	0.51	0.62	0.36	0.87

Table 5. Results on the Seminar Announcement test data with two variants of the
TnT HMM tagger. This and subsequent figures refer to F1 scores.

	Simple	Context
address	0.00	0.00
birthday	0.46	**0.55**
compskill	0.36	**0.37**
degree	0.42	0.42
degreedate	0.39	**0.42**
email	**0.40**	0.33
experience	0.30	**0.32**
experiencedate	0.46	**0.48**
langprofi	0.63	**0.80**
langskill	**0.90**	0.87
marstat	1.00	1.00
military	0.44	**0.57**
name	**0.71**	0.43
phone	0.00	0.00

Table 6. Results on the German CV test data with two variants of the TnT HMM
tagger.

4.2   TK_SemTagger Results

For the feature set of TK_SemTagger, we have experimented with variants of
the feature set shown in Figure 1. This feature template has previous 'tag'

decisions and 'words' in the left context. The right context and the focus word have word features and 'lex' features (ambiguity classes). Moreover, the focus position has a number of wordform-oriented features which allow us to classify unknown words. The weights of these features are shown in Figure 2.

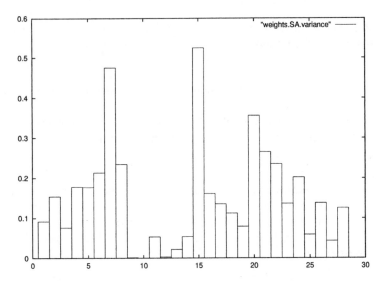

Fig. 2. The feature weights (using the *Shared Variance* statistic in the best setting for the Seminar Announcement data set). The features are the ones shown in Figure 1, ordered per position slot, and sorted alphabetically per slot. The highest weighted feature is the 'lex' feature (15) for the focus word, then the 'tag' of the previous word (7), and then the 'word' in focus position (20).

Context Size. A first set of experiments on the validation set was performed to test the influence of the number of context positions in the feature template. The results for the Seminar Announcement data shown in Table 7. A context size of zero means that only features of the focus word were used, a size of one means that one position to the left and one to the right were used (with both 'word' and 'tag' or 'lex' features).

Without context features (0) the model is quite helpless. One would expect that with an ideal feature weighting method, more context would simply improve performance. This is, unfortunately, not the case, which points to a serious problem of the feature weighting methods used. Because each feature receives a weight, independently of the others, on the basis of its predictiveness for the category, an unwanted effect takes place: highly redundant

context size	speaker	location	stime	etime
0	0.05	0.69	0.01	0.00
1	0.45	0.87	0.92	0.96
2	0.64	0.84	0.91	0.84
3	0.67	0.83	0.93	0.89
4	0.65	0.84	0.93	0.89
5	0.57	0.82	0.95	0.96

Table 7. Experiments on the Seminar Announcement validation data with different context sizes ('word' and 'tag' features; frequency threshold is 4).

features will tend to overwhelm independent but useful features. If we increase the context size, then even when far away context receives much lower weight than close context, the influence of the focus features on the similarity metric will be diluted. In the remainder of the experiments, we use a context size of 4.

Frequency Threshold. Low frequent words can sometimes cause the similarity metric to overestimate the importance of unreliable information. In Table 8, we show the effect of including values for the 'word' feature only for words above a certain frequency threshold. The threshold 4 was chosen for further experiments.

frequency threshold	speaker	location	stime	etime
1	0.41	0.84	0.93	0.89
2	0.55	0.82	0.93	0.89
3	0.65	0.81	0.93	0.89
4	0.65	0.84	0.93	0.89
5	0.63	0.86	0.93	0.89
10	0.48	0.83	0.93	0.89

Table 8. Experiments on the Seminar Announcement validation data with different frequency thresholds for the inclusion of the 'word' feature values.

Decision Propagation. Unlike the HMM, which examines all possible paths through the state space, the current TK_SemTagger has a greedy search strategy. The previous decisions of the tagger are propagated to the left context features. These decisions, however, may be incorrect. However, the model's training set contains correct left context features. Table 9 shows the results of experiments that examine the influence of this effect.

The top row of Table 9, labeled **tags**, shows the normal propagation of tag decisions to the left context. In the second row, labeled **lex**, the left

	speaker	location	stime	etime
tags	0.65	0.84	0.93	0.89
lex	0.43	0.85	0.71	0.29
tags+lex	0.51	0.86	0.93	0.93
bootstrap	0.44	0.83	0.67	0.44
bootstrap+focus	0.42	0.83	0.67	0.44

Table 9. Experiments on the validation set with various propagation types for the left 'tag' context (context size is 4; frequency threshold is 4).

context was constructed using 'lex' features, so no erroneous information is propagated from the classifiers decisions, and the left context patterns are from the same distribution during training and testing. The performance, however, seriously drops. The disambiguated left context is clearly the superior set of predictors, despite the noise. The bad effect of feature-redundancy on the effectivity of weighting is again seen in row three, labeled **tags+lex**. The bottom two rows test the use of a second classifier, identical to the initial one, whose cross-validated output on the training set was used to replace the 'tag' features (**bootstrap**) or to replace the 'tag' features in the context and add a new 'tag' feature for the focus word. Accuracy does not benefit from either of these manipulations.

The categories, or states of the classification-based model were only 'background' and one for each of the types of filler. We experimented briefly with adding prefix and suffix categories like in the TnT Context model, but this only deteriorated performance.

Comparison TK_SemTagger vs TnT. Tables 10 and 11 show the best settings of TnT and TK_SemTagger respectively on the test set of the Seminar Announcements data, and in a ten fold cross validation on the German CV data. The results on the SA task are clearly in favor of the Memory-Based model. The variety of strong cue-phrases in this domain is more easily modeled using 'word' features and a large context size. Similar results have been shown by [17] in their optimization of HMM structures toward this task.

	speaker	location	stime	etime
TK_SemTagger	**0.71**	**0.87**	**0.95**	**0.96**
TnT Context	0.66	0.70	0.85	0.90

Table 10. Best parameter setting for TK_SemTagger, tested on the test set, and compared with the TnT Context model.

The results on the German CV data set are more favorable for the HMM approach. The small size of this data set, its larger set of fillers and the large lexical variety in these fillers seem, so far, to favor the more simple and robust approach.

	TnT Context	TK_ST Best	*Textractor full*
address	0.08	**0.10**	*0.25*
birthday	0.55	0.55	*0.67*
compskill	0.43	0.43	*0.83*
degree	**0.34**	0.29	*0.31*
degreedate	**0.50**	0.35	*0.55*
email	0.53	**0.59**	*0.88*
experience	**0.31**	0.17	*0.38*
experiencedate	**0.42**	0.34	*0.48*
langprofi	**0.60**	0.52	*0.72*
langskill	**0.79**	0.65	*0.87*
marstat	**0.95**	0.87	*0.88*
military	0.58	**0.70**	*0.59*
name	**0.28**	0.21	*0.80*
phone	**0.34**	0.20	*0.84*

Table 11. Comparison between TnT and the best settings of TK_SemTagger in a ten fold cross-validation experiment on the German CV data set. For reference, we have included the results of a somewhat more elaborate system trained by Textkernel on this dataset. This uses a special CV tuned feature set, a combination of HMMs, MBL, and NLP preprocessing (results here are without rule-based post-processing).

5 Discussion and Future Work

We have shown the application of a Memory-Based classification-oriented framework for Information Extraction as an extension of our earlier work in Memory-Based tagging, chunking and shallow parsing. We have compared our approach to Hidden Markov Models and showed competitive or better results. Without denying the robustness and good accuracy of HMMs, we have argued that the feature-rich classification-oriented approach which factors diverse information sources into the feature space, rather than into the state space, offers the potential for future advances in the state of the art, and leads to a more natural way of modeling complex Information Extraction tasks. Similar results can also be achieved with suitable modifications of HMMs. In fact, a number of recently proposed modifications [17,24] which have shown good results have a similar feature-oriented flavor to them. We think it will be possible to borrow the best of the HMM approach, and apply it to the classification-based approach, and *vice versa*. For example, so far, we have lacked the advantage of optimizing the whole sequence of tags probabilistically. Work on this issue is under way. On the other hand, the work on similarity metrics and variations in feature representation that has received a lot of attention in the classification-oriented line of work could very well benefit the further refinement of HMM style models.

In the present paper, we have shown how our approach can easily be implemented in terms of Memory-Based classifiers. This learning framework has a number of important advantages at the moment, most notably its easy implementation, its flexibility with respect to various modeling scenarios, and its low computational complexity during training and classification. However, the Memory-Based approach also suffers from a number of problems, such as the effective weighting of sparse and interacting features, and the current lack of a clear probabilistic interpretation that allows the principled combination of sequences of decisions into larger representations for sequences and hierarchical structures. Several other classification frameworks, such as Maximum Entropy models [2,24], and Conditional Random Fields [22] are explicitly probabilistic, but this advantage is not always translated into higher generalization accuracy. Moreover, other non-probabilistic classifiers such as Support Vector Machines [21], and Winnow perceptrons [25] have also successfully been adopted as semi-probabilistic components in sequence models, so it seems worthwhile at the moment to further investigate this class of learning models both experimentally and theoretically.

References

1. Abney, S. 1996. Part-of-Speech Tagging and Partial Parsing. In K.W. Church, S. Young and G. Bloothooft (eds.), Corpus-Based Methods in Language and Speech. Kluwer Academic Publishers, Dordrecht, 1996.
2. Berger, A., S. Della Pietra, and V. Della Pietra. 1996. Maximum Entropy Approach to Natural Language Processing. *Computational Linguistics*, 22(1).
3. Bikel, D.M., S. Miller, R. Schwartz, and R. Weischedel. 1997. Nymble: a high-performance learning name-finder. In Proceedings of ANLP-97, pp. 194–201.
4. Brants, T. 2000. TnT – a statistical part-of-speech tagger. In Proc. of the 6th Applied NLP Conference, ANLP-2000, April 29 – May 3, 2000, Seattle, WA.
5. Brill, E. 1994. Some advances in transformation-based part-of-speech tagging. In *Proceedings AAAI'94*.
6. Buchholz, S., J.B. Veenstra, and W. Daelemans. 1999. Cascaded Grammatical Relation Assignment. In Proceedings of EMNLP/VLC-99, University of Maryland, USA, June 21-22, 1999, pp. 239-246.
7. Califf, M.E. and R.J. Mooney 1999. Relational Learning of Pattern-Match Rules for Information Extraction. In Proceedings of the Sixteenth National Conference on Artificial Intelligence (AAAI-99), Orlando, FL, pp. 328-334, July 1999.
8. Church, K. W. 1988. A stochastic parts program and noun phrase parser for unrestricted text. In *Proc. of Second Applied NLP (ACL)*.
9. Cohen, W.W. 1995. Fast effective rule induction. In Proceedings of the Twelfth International Conference on Machine Learning, Lake Tahoe, CA, 1995.

10. Daelemans, W., J. Zavrel, P. Berck, and S. Gillis. 1996. MBT: A memory-based part of speech tagger generator. In E. Ejerhed and I. Dagan, editors, *Proc. of Fourth Workshop on Very Large Corpora*, pages 14–27. ACL SIGDAT.

11. Daelemans, W., S. Buchholz, and J. Veenstra. 1999. Memory-Based Shallow Parsing In: Proc, of CoNLL-99, Bergen, Norway, June 12, 1999.

12. Daelemans, W., A. Van den Bosch, and J. Zavrel. 1999. Forgetting exceptions is harmful in language learning. *Machine Learning, Special issue on Natural Language Learning.*

13. Daelemans, W., J. Zavrel, K. Van der Sloot, and A. Van den Bosch. 2001. TiMBL: Tilburg Memory Based Learner, version 4.0, reference manual. Technical Report ILK-0001, ILK, Tilburg University.

14. DeRose, S. 1988. Grammatical category disambiguation by statistical optimization. *Computational Linguistics*, 14:31–39.

15. Freitag, D. Machine Learning for Information Extraction in Informal Domains. PhD. thesis, November, 1998.

16. Freitag D. and A. McCallum. 1999. Information extraction using HMMs and shrinkage. Proceedings of the AAAI-99 Workshop on Machine Learning for Information Extraction.

17. Freitag D. and A. McCallum, "Information extraction with HMM structures learned by stochastic optimization," Proceedings of AAAI-2000.

18. Grefenstette, G. 1996. Light parsing as finite state filtering. In Workshop on Extended finite state models of language, Budapest, Hungary, Aug 11–12 1996. ECAI'96.

19. van Halteren, H., J. Zavrel, and W. Daelemans. 2001. Improving Accuracy in Word Class tagging through the Combination of Machine Learning Systems. *Computational Linguistics*, Vol.27(2).

20. Huffman, S.B. 1996. Learning Information Extraction Patterns from Examples. In Connectionist, Statistical, and Symbolic Approaches to Learning for Natural Language Processing, pp. 246–260. Springer Verlag.

21. Kudoh, T. and Y. Matsumoto. 2001. Chunking with Support Vector Machines. In Proceedings of NAACL 2001, Pittsburgh, PA, USA, 2001.

22. Lafferty, J., A. McCallum, and F. Pereira. 2001. Conditional random fields: Probabilistic models for segmenting and labeling sequence data. In Proceedings of ICML-01, pages 282-289, 2001.

23. Magerman, D.M. 1994. Natural Language Parsing as Statistical Pattern Recognition. PhD Thesis, February 1994.

24. McCallum, A., D. Freitag, and F. Pereira. 2000. Maximum entropy Markov models for information extraction and segmentation. Proceedings of ICML-2000.

25. Punyakanok, V. and D. Roth. 2000. The Use of Classifiers in Sequential Inference. NIPS-13, Dec, 2000.

26. Quinlan, J.R. 1993. C4.5: *Programs for Machine Learning.* San Mateo, CA: Morgan Kaufmann.

27. Rabiner, L.R. 1989. A tutorial on hidden Markov models and selected applications in speech recognition. Proceedings of the IEEE, 77(2), pp. 257–286.

28. Ramshaw, L.A. and Marcus, M.P. 1995. Text Chunking using Transformation-Based Learning. In Third Workshop on Very Large Corpora, ACL, pp. 82-94, 1995.

29. Ratnaparkhi, A. 1996. A maximum entropy part-of-speech tagger. In *Proc. of the Conference on Empirical Methods in Natural Language Processing, May 17-18, 1996, University of Pennsylvania.*
30. Ratnaparkhi, A. 1997. A Linear Observed Time Statistical Parser Based on Maximum Entropy Models. In Proceedings of the Second Conference on Empirical Methods in Natural Language Processing. Aug. 1-2, 1997. Brown University, Providence, RI.
31. Riloff, E. 1993 Automatically Constructing a Dictionary for Information Extraction Tasks. In Proceedings of the Eleventh National Conference on Artificial Intelligence (AAAI-93) , AAAI Press/The MIT Press, pp. 811–816.
32. Soderland, S., D. Fisher, J. Aseltine, and W. Lehnert. 1995. Crystal: Inducing a conceptual dictionary. In Proceedings of the Fourteenth International Joint Conference on Artificial Intelligence, pp. 1314–1319.
33. Zavrel, J. and W. Daelemans. 1997. Memory-based learning: Using similarity for smoothing. In *Proc. of 35th annual meeting of the ACL*, Madrid.
34. Zavrel, J. and W. Daelemans. Bootstrapping a tagged corpus through combination of existing heterogeneous taggers. In Proceedings of the second international conference on language resources and evaluation (LREC-2000), Athens, Greece, 17-20, 2000.

Concept Drift and the Importance of Examples

Ralf Klinkenberg and Stefan Rüping

University of Dortmund
Computer Science Department, Artificial Intelligence Unit (LS VIII)
44221 Dortmund, Germany
{klinkenberg, rueping}@ls8.cs.uni-dortmund.de

http://www-ai.cs.uni-dortmund.de/

Abstract. For many learning tasks where data is collected over an extended period of time, its underlying distribution is likely to change. A typical example is information filtering, i.e. the adaptive classification of documents with respect to a particular user interest. Both the interest of the user and the document content change over time. A filtering system should be able to adapt to such concept changes.

Examples may be important for different reasons. In case of a drifting concept, the importance of an example obviously depends on its age. If a user is interested in several topics, these may be of different importance to her/him. Hence the importance of an example is influenced by the topic it belongs to. Of course these two effects may cumulate.

In this paper we model the importance of an example by weighting its importance for the final decision function. This paper investigates how to handle these two effects with support vector machines extending the approach of [12], which showed that drifting concepts can be learned effectively and efficiently with little parameterization. Several approaches addressing the different effects are compared in experiments on real-world text data.

1 Introduction

Machine learning methods are often applied to problems, where data is collected over an extended period of time. In many real-world applications this introduces the problem that the distribution underlying the data is likely to change over time. For example, companies collect an increasing amount of data like sales figures and customer data to find patterns in the customer behavior and to predict future sales. As the customer behavior tends to change over time, the model underlying successful predictions should be adapted accordingly.

The same problem occurs in information filtering, i.e. the adaptive classification of documents with respect to a particular user interest. Information filtering techniques are used, for example, to build personalized news filters, which learn about the news-reading preferences of a user or to filter e-mail.

Both the interest of the user and the document content change over time. A filtering system should be able to adapt to such concept changes.

In this paper, we discuss several approaches to deal with the problem of concept drift. The central question will be, how important older examples are for predicting new instances of the possibly changed concept. Examples may be important for different reasons. In case of a drifting concept, the importance of an example obviously depends on its age. If a user is interested in several topics, these may be of different importance to her/him. Hence the importance of an example is influenced by the topic it belongs to. Of course these two effects may cumulate.

We will extend the approach of [12] by using some special properties of support vector machines, that will prove useful in handling concept drift, for example efficient performance estimation, transduction, and example weighting. A main goal will be to keep the learning algorithm as effective, efficient, and with as little parameterization as possible. Several approaches addressing the different effects are compared in experiments on real-world text data.

2   Concept Drift

Throughout this paper, we study the problem of concept drift for the pattern recognition problem in the following framework. Each example $z = (x, y)$ consists of a feature vector $x \in \mathbf{R}^N$ and a label $y \in \{-1, +1\}$ indicating its classification. Data arrives over time in batches. Without loss of generality these batches are assumed to be of equal size, each containing m examples.

$$z_{(1,1)}, \ldots, z_{(1,m)}, z_{(2,1)}, \ldots, z_{(2,m)}, \ldots, z_{(t,1)}, \ldots, z_{(t,m)}, z_{(t+1,1)}, \ldots, z_{(t+1,m)}$$

$z_{(i,j)}$ denotes the j-th example of batch i. For each batch i the data is independently identically distributed with respect to a distribution $\Pr_i(x, y)$. Depending on the amount and type of concept drift, the example distribution $\Pr_i(x, y)$ and $\Pr_{i+1}(x, y)$ between batches will differ. The goal of the learner $\mathcal{L}$ is to sequentially predict the labels of the next batch. For example, after batch t the learner can use any subset of the training examples from batches 1 to t to predict the labels of batch $t + 1$. The learner aims to minimize the cumulated number of prediction errors. In machine learning, changing concepts are often handled by time windows of fixed or adaptive size on the training data [19,30,16,13] or by weighting data or parts of the hypothesis according to their age and/or utility for the classification task [15,27]. The latter approach of weighting examples has already been used for information filtering in the incremental relevance feedback approaches of [1] and [2]. In this paper, the earlier approach maintaining a window of adaptive size is explored. More detailed descriptions of the methods described above and further approaches can be found in [10].

For windows of fixed size, the choice of a *"good" window size* is a compromise between fast adaptivity (small window) and good generalization in phases without concept change (large window). The basic idea of *adaptive window management* is to adjust the window size to the current extent of concept drift.

The task of learning drifting or time-varying concepts has also been studied in computational learning theory. Learning a changing concept is infeasible, if no restrictions are imposed on the type of admissible concept changes,[1] but drifting concepts are provably efficiently learnable (at least for certain concept classes), if the rate or the extent of drift is limited in particular ways.

Helmbold and Long [5] assume a possibly permanent but slow concept drift and define the *extent of drift* as the probability that two subsequent concepts disagree on a randomly drawn example. Their results include an upper bound for the extend of drift maximally tolerable by any learner and algorithms that can learn concepts that do not drift more than a certain constant extent of drift. Furthermore they show that it is sufficient for a learner to see a fixed number of the most recent examples. Hence a window of a certain minimal fixed size allows to learn concepts for which the extent of drift is appropriately limited.

While Helmbold and Long restrict the extend of drift, Kuh, Petsche, and Rivest [14] determine a maximal *rate of drift* that is acceptable by any learner, i. e. a maximally acceptable frequency of concept changes, which implies a lower bound for the size of a fixed window for a time-varying concept to be learnable, which is similar to the lower bound of Helmbold and Long.

In practice, however, it usually cannot be guaranteed that the application at hand obeys these restrictions, e.g. a reader of electronic news may change his interests (almost) arbitrarily often and radically. Furthermore the large time window sizes, for which the theoretical results hold, would be impractical. Hence more application oriented approaches rely on far smaller windows of fixed size or on window adjustment heuristics that allow far smaller window sizes and usually perform better than fixed and/or larger windows [30,16,13]. While these heuristics are intuitive and work well in their particular application domain, they usually require tuning their parameters, are often not transferable to other domains, and lack a proper theoretical foundation.

Sayed, Liu, and Sung [26] describe an approach to incrementally learning support vector machines that handles *virtual* concept drift implied by incrementally learning from several subsamples of a large training set, but they do not address the problem of (*real*) concept drift addressed here.

3   Support Vector Machines

We use support vector machines as our learning algorithm, because SVMs have some very useful properties that can be exploited in our approach. The theory of SVMs itself is well known (see [29]), therefore we will give only a

---

[1] E.g. a function randomly jumping between the values one and zero cannot be predicted by any learner with more than 50% accuracy.

short introduction of the concepts that are important with respect to our work.

Support vector machines are based on the structural risk minimization principle [29] of statistical learning theory. Statistical learning theory deals with the question, how a function f from a class of functions $(f_\alpha)_{\alpha \in \Lambda}$ can be found, that minimizes the expected risk

$$R[f] = \int \int L(y, f(x)) dP(y|x) dP(x) \tag{1}$$

with respect to a loss function L, when the distributions of the examples $P(x)$ and their classifications $P(y|x)$ are unknown and have to be estimated from finitely many examples $(x_i, y_i)_{i \in I}$.

The SVM algorithm solves this problem by minimizing the regularized risk $R_{\text{reg}}[f]$, which is the weighted sum of the empirical risk $R_{\text{emp}}[f]$ with respect to the data $(x_i, y_i)_{i=1...n}$ and a complexity term $||w||^2$

$$R_{\text{reg}}[f] = ||w||^2 + C \cdot R_{\text{emp}}[f]. \tag{2}$$

In their basic formulation, support vector machines find a linear decision function $y = f(x) = \text{sign}(w \cdot x + b)$ that both minimizes the prediction error on the training set and promises the best generalization performance. Geometrically the principle of the SVM can be interpreted as finding a hyperplane in the example space, that separates the positive and negative examples (minimizes the error on the training set) with maximum margin (best generalization performance), see Figure 1.

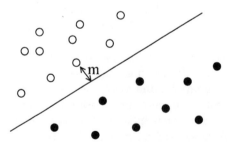

Fig. 1. Maximum margin hyperplane and margin m.

Given the examples $(x_1, y_1), \ldots, (x_n, y_n)$ the SVM solution is found by solving the following optimization problem:

$$\Psi(w, \xi) = \frac{1}{2}(w^T w) + C \sum_{i=1}^{n} \xi_i \tag{3}$$
$$\rightarrow \min$$

subject to

$$y_i(w^T x_i + b) \leq 1 - \xi_i, i = 1, \ldots, n \tag{4}$$

$$\xi_i \geq 0, i = 1, \ldots, n \tag{5}$$

The decision hyperplane is given by the normal vector w and the additive constant b, such that $f(x) = w^T x + b$. The variables ξ_i are slack variables that allow for a certain amount of misclassification in equation (4). In practice, this optimization problem can be efficiently solved in its dual form

$$\Phi(\alpha) = -\frac{1}{2} \sum_{i,j=1}^{n} y_i y_j x_i \cdot x_j + \sum_{i=1}^{n} \alpha_i \tag{6}$$
$$\rightarrow \min$$

subject to

$$0 \leq \alpha_i \leq C \quad \forall i = 1 \ldots n \tag{7}$$

$$\sum_{i=1}^{n} \alpha_i = 0 \tag{8}$$

Here, the hyperplane is given by $w = \sum_{i=1}^{n} \alpha_i y_i x_i$. The vectors x_i that have non-zero variables α_i are called the support vectors. The so-called capacity constant C limits the maximum impact an individual example may have on the hypothesis to be learned and thereby allows to trade off model complexity versus generalization.

3.1   Loss Functions

In equation (3), the empirical risk of the SVM solution is measured with respect to a linear loss function, but the support vector algorithm is not restricted to the case of linear loss functions, but can be extended to broader classes of loss functions (e.g. see [25]). In particular, one can set an individual weight c_i to each example by replacing definition (3) by

$$\Psi(w, \xi) = \frac{1}{2}(w^T w) + C \sum_{i=1}^{n} c_i \xi_i. \tag{9}$$

This leads to the same dual formulation as before, except that equation (7) is replaced by

$$0 \leq \alpha_i \leq c_i C \quad \forall i = 1 \ldots n \tag{10}$$

The resulting decision function is biased towards examples with a higher weight. The effect of this manipulation can be viewed as changing the probability distribution $P(x)$ of the examples, placing more probability mass to the examples with higher weight.

3.2   SVMs for Text Classification

It was first noted by Joachims in [6], that SVMs are especially well suited for text classification, because the complexity of a SVM hyperplane depends on the margin it separates the data with and not on the dimensionality of the input space. Text data typically has a very high dimension (more than 10000) and very few irrelevant features. SVMs can efficiently learn with all features in the data set, so they are much better suited than other algorithm that demand complicated feature selection. Experience shows support vector machines are currently the most successful tool for text classification [9].

4   The Importance of Examples

In a learning problem with drifting concepts as introduced in section 2, we face the problem to decide, how much information from past examples can be used to find a hypothesis that is adequate to predict the class information of future data. Since we do not know, if and when a concept drift happens, there are two opposing effects: On the one hand, the older the data is, the more likely it is that its probability distribution differs from the current distribution that underlies the process, so that the data may be misleading. On the other hand, the more data is used in the learning process, the better the results are if no concept drift occurred since the data arrived.

In this section we present different approaches for learning drifting concepts, that differ in the way previous examples are used to construct a new hypothesis. All our approaches share the assumption, that concept drifts do not reverse, i.e. newer examples are always more important than older ones.

This assumption was implemented by a common scheme for estimating the performance of a learner: In all experiments, the performance was only calculated on the last batch of data, regardless of how many batches were used in training. To get a good estimation of the performance but still be efficient, we used the so-called $\xi\alpha$-estimator of [8], which estimates the leave-one-out-error of a SVM based solely on the one SVM solution learned with all examples.

4.1   Example Selection

One of the simplest scenarios for detecting concept drift are concept drifts that happen very quickly between relatively stable single concepts. For example, imagine a user of an information filtering system, who wants to buy a new car: at first, he is interested in information about all sorts of cars, but after he made his decision and bought the car, he is only interested in information about this special type of car. This may be more accurately called "concept change" or "concept shift" rather than "concept drift".

In this scenario, the problem of learning drifting concepts can be approached as the problem of finding the time point t at which the last concept change happened. After that, a standard learning algorithm for fixed concepts can be used to learn from the data since t. Similarly, other concept drift scenarios can be handled by using a time window on the training data, assuming that the amount of drift increases with time and hence focusing on the last n training examples.

The shortcomings of previous windowing approaches are that they either fix the window size [19] or involve complicated heuristics [13,16,30]. A fixed window size makes strong assumptions about how quickly the concept changes. While heuristics can adapt to different speed and amount of drift, they involve many parameters that are difficult to tune.

In [12], Klinkenberg and Joachims presented an approach to selecting an appropriate window size that does not involve complicated parameterization. They key idea is to select the window size so that the estimated generalization error on new examples is minimized. To get an estimate of the generalization error, a special form of $\xi\alpha$-estimates [8] is used. $\xi\alpha$-estimates are a particularly efficient method for estimating the performance of an SVM.

The window adaptive window approach employs these estimates in the following way. At batch t, it essentially tries various window sizes, training a SVM for each resulting training set.

$$z_{(t,1)}, \ldots, z_{(t,m)} \tag{11}$$

$$z_{(t-1,1)}, \ldots, z_{(t-1,m)}, z_{(t,1)}, \ldots, z_{(t,m)} \tag{12}$$

$$z_{(t-2,1)}, \ldots, z_{(t-2,m)}, z_{(t-1,1)}, \ldots, z_{(t-1,m)}, z_{(t,1)}, \ldots, z_{(t,m)} \tag{13}$$

$$\vdots$$

For each window size it computes a $\xi\alpha$-estimate based on the result of training, considering only the last batch for the estimation, that is the m most recent training examples $z_{(t,1)}, \ldots, z_{(t,m)}$

$$Err_{\xi\alpha}^m(h_{\mathcal{L}}) = \frac{|\{i : 1 \leq i \leq m \wedge (\alpha_{(t,i)} R_\Delta^2 + \xi_{(t,i)}) \geq 1\}|}{m} \tag{14}$$

This reflects the assumption that the most recent examples are most similar to the new examples in batch $t + 1$. The window size minimizing the $\xi\alpha$-estimate of the error rate is selected by the algorithm and used to train a classifier for the current batch.

The window adaptation algorithm can be summarized as follows:

- input: a training sample S_{train} consisting of t batches containing m (labeled) examples each
- for $h \in \{0, ..., t-1\}$
    - train SVM on examples $z_{(t-h,1)}, \ldots, z_{(t,m)}$
    - compute $\xi\alpha$-estimate on examples $z_{(t,1)}, \ldots, z_{(t,m)}$
- output: window size which minimizes $\xi\alpha$-estimate

4.2   Example Weighting

In information filtering systems, the user may change his interests in a specific topic slowly. In this case, one cannot find a specific time point, at which old examples become irrelevant, but the amount of information one can draw from a certain example will slowly decrease over a longer amount of time. Therefore, the sharp distinction between examples that are kept and examples that are left out in the learning process does not sufficiently represent the process behind the data.

The decreasing importance of older examples can be modeled by assigning a weight c_i to each example z_i and by learning a decision function with respect to these weights, for example by the method shown in section 3.1.

But how to choose these weights? Of course, a weighting scheme must take into account the variability of the target concept and be adaptive with respect to the actual performance of the learner.

In our approach, the criterion to select the optimal weights is again the estimated performance of the learner on the newest batch of data. This guarantees, that the temporal order of the examples is respected by the weighting schemes (an example from a newly emerging concept looks like an outlier with respect to the old data, but of course is no outlier but highly informative).

In the weighting scheme, we select the weights of the examples solely based on their respective age, for example using an exponential aging function $w_\lambda(x) = \exp(-\lambda t_x)$, where example x was found t_x time steps ago. The larger λ is, the sooner an examples becomes irrelevant. In the extreme cases, for $\lambda \to \infty$ we learn only on the newest examples and for $\lambda = 0$ all examples share an equal weight.

To be adaptive, we start several learning runs for each new batch with different values of λ and pick the best λ at each batch by estimating the performance of the learning result on the last batch of data. In a way, this algorithm is a continuous version of the algorithm of [12] that was presented in the last section: instead of a hard cut to remove uninformative examples, the contribution of these examples to the final learning result is slowly reduced.

4.3   Local Models

A special characteristic of text classification is the high dimensionality of the examples compared to the number of examples, which makes the examples stand almost orthogonal to each other. This is the reason why in text classification tasks the classes often are linearly separable.

In the concept drift setting, we have a set of topics and assume that the user is interested in a specific subset of topics. In experiments with this setting, one can observe that a subset of multiple topics can be separated from the rest of the data just as good as a single topic. Accordingly, one can also observe, that a SVM classifier that is trained in a concept drift setting, even if it is trained on a small subset of the data, has a low error

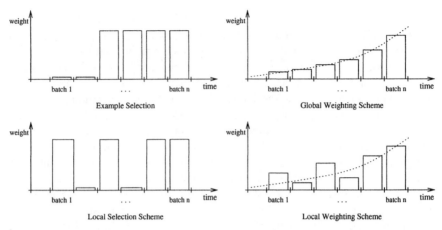

Fig. 2. Comparison of the example weights in the four weighting schemes.

on a test set from the same example distribution (in our experiments, below 10%). Vice versa, if a concept drift occurs, i. e. if the users interest in a topic changes, almost all of the examples from this topic will be classified falsely and the error rate will grow considerably (with the increase of the error rate depending on the size of this topic in relation to the other topics). A good example of this behavior can be seen in Figure 3. In this setting, we can see a considerable increase in the classification error after a concept drift occurs at batch 10. In this example, the classifier was re-trained for each new batch on all examples prior to the new batch.

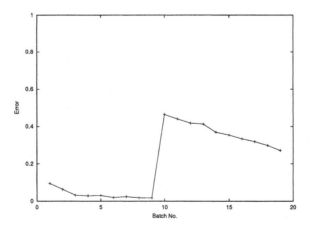

Fig. 3. Typical classification error in a concept drift setting.

This observations lead us to the local model approach: In the first step, a classifier is learned on only the most recent batch of data. Of course, in most cases this classifier will not be as good as it can be, but we can be sure that it always will be the classifier that is most up-to-date with the drifting concept. Now we can use this classifier to estimate, which batches of data were generated from the same model (i. e. the same users interest) as the most recent batch, by comparing the estimated leave-one-out error of the classifier on the most recent batch to its test error on the other batches. The higher the error, the more unlikely is the data given the model. Note that at this point, it is important to use the $\xi\alpha$-estimation and not the training error to avoid errors by over-fitting the most recent data.

In a second step, the information about the error of the classifier can be used to build a training set for the actual classifier. There are two ways to use this information: We can either exclude all batches from the new training set, which have a significantly higher classification error than the most recent batch. By this, we hope to train the final classifier on all data generated by the current model in a way similar to the *example selection scheme* in section 4.1. We can also use the error information to adjust the weights for the examples on each batch in a way similar to section 4.2. The higher the error of the batch, the lower the weights will be. We call this approach the *local weighting scheme*, because here the weights are adjusted locally on each batch in contrast to the *global weighting scheme* in section 4.2. Figure 2 illustrates these different example selection and weighting schemes. Of course, we can also combine both weighting schemes by multiplying the two weights for each example (*combined weighting scheme*). In the spirit of Bayesian statistics, this combines an a-priori assumption about the importance of the examples (the global weight) with an a-posteriori update (performance measure in the local weight).

4.4   Transduction

Transductive learning [29] differs from inductive learning in that its goal is not to find a hypothesis which is optimal with respect to all data, i.e. the real probability distribution of the examples, but to only find a hypothesis which is optimal for a given test set. That is, transductive learning does not only learn from a given example set, but also from a set of observations (without given classification), whose values are to be predicted. Transduction can improve the performance of the learner considerably, since a much better estimation of the distribution of the observations $P(x)$ can be obtained from the training and test set together (of course, $P(y|x)$ can be only estimated on the training set).

In [7], Joachims shows that the principle of transductive learning is very well suited for the problem of text classification. For example, in information retrieval systems the collection of all available documents is usually known, but the user can only label a very small fraction of all documents as being relevant or not relevant. In the same publication, Joachims also shows how transductive learning can be efficiently performed with SVMs.

Empirical results (see e.g. [7,18,21]) show that unlabeled data can help to significantly improve the performance of text classifiers, especially in case of few labeled examples. As pointed out in [7], it is well known in information retrieval that words in natural language occur in strong co-occurrence patterns (see [28]). While some words are likely to occur in one document, others are not. This type of information is independent of the document labels and can be exploited, if unlabeled data is used.

Transduction and Concept Drift. Transductive learning has also been applied to the setting of concept drift by Klinkenberg in [11] using the following idea. At each batch, there are usually only comparatively few observations, for which predictions need to be made. Since the performance improvements achieved by transduction are the more significant the more data is used, only using such a small set of unlabeled data does not seem optimal. But the out-of-date examples, whose labels do no longer seem to be representative enough for the current concept, and may be some other unlabeled examples from the same source are still available. Assuming that the process that generated the data (e.g. the news stream) is still approximately the same and that only the user's preferences in what is relevant to him or her changed, the x-values of this examples can be used as unclassified observation for transductive learning. In this way, even for very new topics with little examples, a large collection of documents can be used to estimate $P(x)$.

Klinkenberg [11] describes an extension of [12] (see also section 4.1) exploiting unlabeled and old no longer reliably labeled data in such a transductive way. Its basic idea is to first use the algorithm described in [12] to find a good window size on the labeled training data, $win_{labeled}$, using $\xi\alpha$-estimates for an inductive SVM. Then an almost identical algorithm is used to determine a good window size on the unlabeled data, $win_{unlabeled}$, on the same stream of documents for a transductive SVM, leaving the window size $win_{labeled}$ unchanged.

Why are separate window sizes $win_{labeled}$ and $win_{unlabeled}$ maintained for labeled and unlabeled data respectively? The probability $P(y|x)$, which describes the user interest, i.e. the drifting concept, and which is captured by the labeled data, may change at an other rate than the probability $P(x)$, which describes the distribution of documents identically underlying both the labeled and unlabeled examples independent of their labels. While the window on the labeled data tries to capture a training set representative for $P(y|x)$, the window on the unlabeled data tries to find a possibly larger set of examples representative for $P(x)$. Hence it is sensible to use separate windows to obtain the best information from both probability distributions. This may be particularly helpful in cases where the user interest changes much faster or more often than the underlying document distribution.

The algorithm to find the window for the unlabeled data (and the final hypothesis) can be summarized as follows:

- input: a training sample S_{train} consisting of t batches containing m' examples each and a test sample S_{test}
- for $h \in \{0, ..., t-1\}$
  - train TSVM on examples $z_{(t-h,1)}, ..., z_{(t,m')}$, considering all training examples outside the window of size $win_{labeled}$ as unlabeled, and on the test examples $z_{(t+1,1)}, ..., z_{(t+1,m')}$
  - compute $\xi\alpha$-estimate on examples $z_{(t+1,1)}, ..., z_{(t+1,m')}$
- output: window size which minimizes $\xi\alpha$-estimate ($win_{unlabeled}$)

Other Approaches to Exploiting Unlabeled Data. Besides of transduction, there are also other (semi-)supervised approaches for exploiting unlabeled data. Nigam et al. [20,21] use a multinomial Naive Bayes classifier and incorporate unlabeled data using the EM-algorithm. One problem with using Naive Bayes is that its independence assumption is clearly violated for text. Nevertheless, using EM showed substantial improvements over the performance of a regular Naive Bayes classifier. Lanquillon [18] describes an extension of this EM-based framework to an EM-style framework for arbitrary (text) classifiers.

Blum and Mitchell's work on co-training [3] uses unlabeled data in a particular setting. They exploit the fact that, for some problems, each example can be described by multiple representations. WWW-pages, for example, can be represented as the text on the page and/or the anchor texts on the hyperlinks pointing to this page. Blum and Mitchell develop a boosting scheme which exploits a conditional independence between these representations.

One of the situations, in which a user may change his or her preferences, may occur, when the documents available to the user change, i.e. when the distribution $P(x)$ changes. Lanquillon [17] presents an approach to make use of unlabeled data for the detection of concept drift in such situations.

4.5 Multiple Topics

Until now, we only talked about relevant and irrelevant examples without any further distinction. But in reality, a set of documents (news article, newsgroup postings, emails,...) will contain a whole set of topics and there usually will be more than one relevant topic, for example business email and private email in contrast to spam (of course, in reality the topics will be much more fine-grained).

In the usual task of text classification with fixed concepts, this is not a major problem, because it can be observed that due to the very high dimension it is usually possible to separate multiple relevant topics from the remaining texts as well as it is with single topics.

The difference of multiple topics with concept drift is, that different topics usually will not become relevant or irrelevant at the same time. For examples, if the user takes another job, the relevance of a certain business email may drastically change, but the relevance of private email will still be the same.

In this situation it may help to cluster the documents beforehand and to learn on each cluster separately. The final decision rule will be to mark an examples as relevant, if any of the individual decision rules marks this example as relevant.

The performance of this approach depends largely on the quality of the results of the clustering algorithm. Not only do we need meaningful clusters, we also need clusters that remain stable over time. We can hope to find these clusters, if the distribution $P(x)$ remains constant and only $P(y|x)$, i.e. the users interest, changes. In all other cases, the clustering will have to be repeated from time to time.

5 Experiments

5.1 Experimental Setup

In order to evaluate the learning approaches for drifting concepts proposed in this paper, three simple non-adaptive data management approaches are compared to the adaptive time window approach and to the example weighting and selection strategies, all using SVMs as their core learning algorithm:

- *"Full Memory"*: The learner generates its classification model from all previously seen examples, i.e. it cannot "forget" old examples.
- *"No Memory"*: The learner always induces its hypothesis only from the most recent batch. This corresponds to using a window of the fixed size of one batch.
- Window of *"Fixed Size"*: A time window of the fixed size of three batches is used on the training data. This fixed size outperformed smaller and larger fixed window sizes in the following experiments.
- Window of *"Adaptive Size"*: The window adjustment algorithm [12] proposed in section 4.1 adapts the window size to the current concept drift situation.
- *"Global Weights"*: The examples of old batches are weighted by an exponential aging function according to their age, so that older example receive lower weights (see section 4.2).
- *"Local Weights"*: The examples of old batches are weighted according to their fit to a model learned on the most recent batch only, i.e. the weight of an example x of an old batch t_x is inversely proportional to the error rate of that batch on this model: $w_{local}(x) := 1 - 5 \cdot (error_{t_x} - 0.1)$, where the weight is set to one for error rates below 10% and to zero for error rates above 30% (see section 4.3).

68   Klinkenberg, Rüping

- *"Batch Selection"*: The batches producing an error less than twice the estimated error of the newest batch, when applied to a model learned on the newest batch only, receive a weight of one. The weight of all other examples is set to zero.

The experiments are performed in an information filtering domain, a typical application area for learning drifting concept. Text documents are represented as attribute-value vectors (*bag of words* model), where each distinct word corresponds to a feature whose value is the "ltc"-TF/IDF-weight [24] of that word in that document. Words occurring less than three times in the training data or occurring in a given list of stop words are not considered. Each document feature vector is normalized to unit length to abstract from different document lengths.

The performance of a classifier is measured by the three metrics prediction error, recall, and precision. *Recall* is the probability, that the classifier recognizes a relevant document as relevant. *Precision* is the probability, that a document classified as relevant actually is relevant. All reported results are estimates averaged over four runs.

The experiments use a subset of 2608 documents of the data set of the *Text REtrieval Conference (TREC)* consisting of English business news texts. Each text is assigned to one or several categories. The categories considered here are 1 (Antitrust Cases Pending), 3 (Joint Ventures), 4 (Debt Rescheduling), 5 (Dumping Charges), and 6 (Third World Debt Relief). For the experiments, three concept change scenarios are simulated. The texts are randomly split into 20 batches of equal size containing 130 documents each.[2] The texts of each category are distributed as equally as possible over the 20 batches.

In the three scenarios, a document is considered relevant at a certain point in time, if it matches the interest of the simulated user at that time. For each TREC topic and each batch in each scenario the probability that a document from this topic is relevant for the user interest at this time (batch) is specified. In the scenarios simulated here, the user interest changes between the topics 1 and 3. Documents of the classes 4, 5, and 6 are never relevant in any of these scenarios. Figure 4 shows the probability of being relevant for a document of category 1 at each batch for each of the three scenarios. Documents of category 3 are specified to always have the inverse relevance probability of documents of category 1, i.e. *1 - relevance of category 1*. In the first scenario (*scenario A*), first documents of category 1 are considered relevant for the user interest and all other documents irrelevant. This changes abruptly (concept shift) in batch 10, where documents of category 3 are relevant and all others irrelevant. In the second scenario (*scenario B*), again first documents of category 1 are considered relevant for the user interest and all other documents irrelevant. This changes slowly (concept drift) from batch 8 to batch 12, where documents of category 3 are relevant and all others

---

[2] Hence, in each trial, out of the 2608 documents, eight randomly selected texts are not considered.

irrelevant. The third scenario (*scenario C*) simulates an abrupt concept shift in the user interest from category 1 to category 3 in batch 9 and back to category 1 in batch 11.

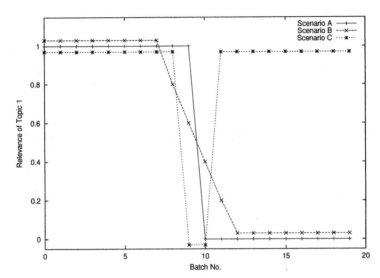

Fig. 4. Relevance of the TREC topic 1 in the concept change scenarios A, B, and C. The relevance of TREC topic 3 is *1 - relevance of topic 1*. The relevance of all other topics is always zero.

The experiments were conducted with the machine learning environment YALE [4,22].[3] For all time window, example weighting, and example selection approaches support vector machines were used as core learning algorithm. Here we chose the SVM implementation *mySVM* [23].[4] Since linear kernels are the standard kernel type used for text classification problems, and since more complex kernel types usually do not perform better on text classification tasks, only linear and no other kernel types were tried here. After preliminary experiments to determine a good value for the capacity constant C of the SVM, which allows to trade off model complexity versus generalization, testing the values $C \in \{1, 10, 100, 1000\}$, the value $C = 1000$ was chosen for the experiments described here.

For the global weighting scheme, an exponential aging function of the form $w_\lambda(x) = \exp(-\lambda t_x)$, where example x was found t_x time steps ago, was employed unless mentioned otherwise. At each batch, the value of the param-

---

[3] YALE: available at http://yale.cs.uni-dortmund.de/

[4] *mySVM*: available at http://www-ai.cs.uni-dortmund.de/SOFTWARE/MYSVM/

eter λ is automatically chosen among $\lambda \in \{0.01, 0.1, 0.2, 0.4, 0.6, 1.0, 2.0, 4.0\}$, such that the chosen value optimizes the expected performance of the learner.

5.2 Experimental Results

Table 1 shows the results of all time window, example weighting, and batch selection approaches on all scenarios in terms of the metrics prediction error, recall, and precision. While the example weighting methods outperform the trivial non-adaptive approaches, the adaptive time window approach and the batch selection strategy clearly outperform both, the non-adaptive approaches and the example weighting methods.

Figures 5 to 8 compare the prediction error rates of all strategies on scenario A over time, i.e. the graphs depict the prediction error on the following batch for each point in time. Figure 5 shows the error rates of the trivial non-adaptive methods full memory, no memory, and fixed size. Figure 6 presents the error rates of the example weighting methods global and local weighting. Figure 7 compares the example selection strategies using an adaptive time window and batch selection, respectively, and Figure 8 finally compares the best approach of each of the previous groups of strategies.

Table 1. Error, recall, and precision of all time window, example weighting, and example selection methods for all scenarios averaged over 4 trials with 20 batches.

	Full Memory	No Memory	Fixed Size	Global Weights	Local Weights	Adaptive Size	Batch Selection
Scen. A:							
Error	21.11%	11.16%	9.03%	8.45%	8.98%	6.65%	6.15%
Recall	46.70%	52.59%	70.39%	73.75%	73.81%	77.90%	80.24%
Precision	64.66%	91.71%	87.64%	87.64%	85.92%	91.57%	91.73%
Scen. B:							
Error	21.30%	12.64%	9.76%	10.62%	12.29%	9.06%	9.33%
Recall	43.89%	46.81%	65.91%	65.72%	64.16%	68.72%	69.85%
Precision	64.05%	89.74%	87.14%	84.82%	81.36%	88.06%	87.90%
Scen. C:							
Error	8.60%	12.73%	11.19%	8.80%	8.78%	8.56%	7.55%
Recall	71.14%	35.38%	58.30%	68.57%	71.15%	68.97%	74.84%
Precision	83.28%	88.66%	78.84%	84.29%	82.59%	86.65%	87.79%

Among the two example selection strategies, batch selection performs better than the adaptive time window approach, especially on scenario C as Table 1 and Figure 9 show, where the initial concept reflecting the user interest, topic 1, is only shortly interrupted by a concept shift to topic 3, and then returns to topic 1 again. In the batches after the second concept shift in scenario C, the adaptive time window can only capture the data after the second concept shift, if it is to exclude the no longer representative data between the two concept shifts, while the batch selection strategy can also use the earlier data of the time before the first concept shift and selectively exclude only the no longer relevant batches between the two concept shifts. This allows the batch selection to maintain a larger consistent training set and thereby to better generalize resulting in a lower error rate.

From the results of the non-adaptive approaches (full memory, no memory, and fixed size), we can see that the error is the lowest if the time window contains all time points from the current model and no others. For example in scenario A, as depicted in Figure 5, as long as no concept drift occurs, the full memory approach has the lowest error. Immediately after the concept drift the no memory approach quickly returns to its previous error level, while the fixed size memory approach takes longer until it finally reaches a lower error than the no memory approach again. For the full memory approach, even nine time points after the concept shift the error rate is still three times higher than the error of the other strategies. Of course, these findings are not very surprising.

For practical use, though, these non-adaptive approaches are not very useful, as it cannot be determined beforehand, when and how often a concept shift will occur, so an optimal static time window cannot be set. The longer the time window is, the lower error the classifier can achieve if no concept drift occurs, but the shorter the time window is, the faster it will adjust to a new concept. In general, balancing between the two extremes of no and full memory, the fixed size approach seems to work best.

The performance of the example weighting approaches was slightly better than that of the non-adaptive time window approaches. The selection of the weighting parameter gives the algorithm the ability to better adapt to concept changes. As can be seen in Figure 6, the different weighting approaches all had very similar results. Unfortunately, as closer inspection of the weighting parameters chosen by the algorithm shows, there seems to be no pattern in the parameters in relation to the occurrence or absence of concept drift, so it is questionable if the performance of this approach is a result of a better model of the importance of the examples over time.

As an alternative to the exponential weighting function used for the example weighting approaches in the experiments described above, one may use different functions. In order to assess the influence of this choice, we also tried the same experiments using a sigmoidal weighting function instead the exponential one. Assuming that the batches are consecutively numbered with increasing numbers and that the newest batch of labeled examples has the number t_0, the weight of an old batch with the number $t < t_0$ is given by the function $tanh((t - a)/b) + 1)$, where the best combination of the two parameters a and b is automatically selected from the following two value sets $a \in \{1.00 \cdot t_0, 0.85 \cdot t_0, 0.68 \cdot t_0, 0.50 \cdot t_0\}$ and $b \in$

$\{0.01 \cdot t_0, 0.10 \cdot t_0, 0.30 \cdot t_0, 0.60 \cdot t_0, 5.00 \cdot t_0\}$ at each batch, so that the expected error of the final model learned on all batches is minimized on the newest batch. Interestingly, the results for the sigmoidal weighting scheme do not significantly differ from those of the exponential weighting scheme, and hence are not reported in detail here. This may be an indication that weighting examples is not an appropriate model for concept drift in this case.

The adaptive window and the batch selection approach adjust very well to concept drift. In all three scenarios, the error rate quickly reaches its prior level after a concept drift occurred. In scenario C, the batch selection approach outperforms the adaptive window method, as the more flexible way of selecting the final training set allows it to exclude the two outlier batches and use all other data, while the adaptive window method can only use the information before the first concept shift if it also includes the outliers in the middle.

Summing up, the batch selection strategy achieves the lowest error of all tested approaches (Figure 8). An explanation for this may be, that outliers, even if there a relatively few and they receive a low weight, seriously hurt the performance of the SVM classification. As the special properties of text data - very high dimensionality and linear separability - make it easy to identify large groups of outliers, the batch selection method can reliably choose the largest possible set of training examples that are useful to construct the final hypothesis.

6   Summary and Conclusions

In this paper, we proposed several methods for handling concept drift with support vector machines using different strategies to account for the different importance of examples to the current target concept to be learned, where the importance of an example may depend on its age or its topic, and where also unlabeled documents may have an impact.

We extended the approach of [12] by using some special properties of SVMs useful in handling concept drift, for example efficient performance estimation, transduction, and example weighting, keeping the learning algorithm as effective, efficient, and with as little parameterization as possible. Several approaches addressing the different effects were compared in experiments on real-world text data.

Summarizing the results of the concept drift experiments in this information filtering domain, one can observe that example selection by an adaptive time window or by batch selection seems to work better than a gradual weighting scheme depending on the age of and/or performance on the training examples. The importance of an example can easily and successfully be expressed by including it in or excluding it from the training set. A continuously valued representation of the importance or fit of the example does not provide additional useful information.

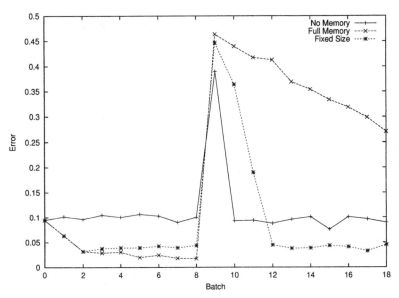

Fig. 5. Classification errors of the trivial approaches on each batch in scenario A (averaged over 4 runs).

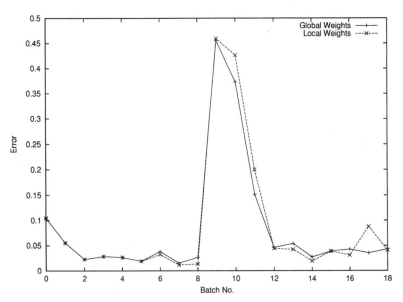

Fig. 6. Classification errors of the weighting approaches on each batch in scenario A (averaged over 4 runs).

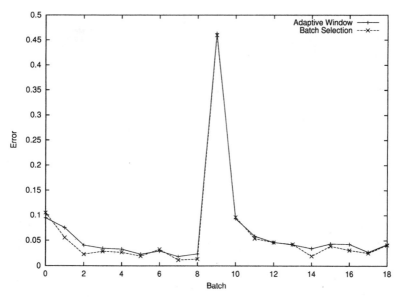

Fig. 7. Classification errors of the batch selection approaches on each batch in scenario A (averaged over 4 runs).

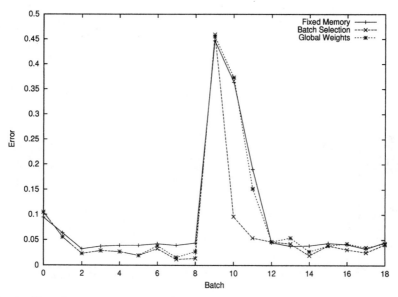

Fig. 8. Classification errors of the best approaches of each type on each batch in scenario A (averaged over 4 runs).

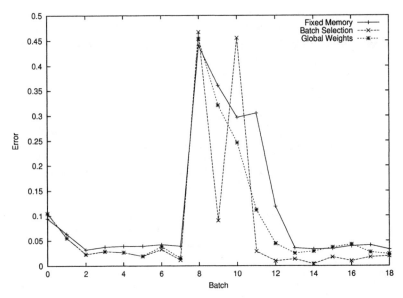

Fig. 9. Classification errors of the best approaches of each type on each batch in scenario C (averaged over 4 runs).

It remains to be investigated, how much the reported results depend the special properties of text data and the way the concept drift scenarios were simulated. In order to judge the transferability of the proposed approaches to other concept drift problems, experiments on further domains with different properties are needed.

Acknowledgments

The financial support of the Deutsche Forschungsgemeinschaft (Collaborative Research Centers SFB 475, "Reduction of Complexity for Multivariate Data Structures", and SFB 531, "Computational Intelligence") is gratefully acknowledged.

References

1. James Allan. Incremental relevance feedback for information filtering. In H. P. Frei, editor, *Proceedings of the Nineteenth ACM Conference on Research and Development in Information Retrieval*, pages 270–278, New York, NY, USA, 1996. ACM Press.
2. Marko Balabanovic. An adaptive web page recommendation service. In W. L. Johnson, editor, *Proceedings of the First International Conference on Autonomous Agents*, pages 378–385, New York, NY, USA, 1997. ACM Press.

3. Avrim Blum and Tom Mitchell. Combining labeled and unlabeled data with co-training. In Peter Bartlett and Yishay Mansour, editors, *Proceedings of the Eleventh Annual Conference on Computational Learning Theory (COLT-98)*, pages 92–100, New York, NY, USA, 1998. ACM Press.
4. Simon Fischer, Ralf Klinkenberg, Ingo Mierswa, and Oliver Ritthoff. YALE: Yet Another Learning Environment - Tutorial. Technical Report CI-136/02, Collaborative Research Center 531 (SFB 531 *Computational Intelligence*), University of Dortmund, Germany, 2002. *http://yale.cs.uni-dortmund.de/*.
5. David P. Helmbold and Philip M. Long. Tracking drifting concepts by minimizing disagreements. *Machine Learning*, 14(1):27–45, 1994.
6. Thorsten Joachims. Text categorization with support vector machines: Learning with many relevant features. In Claire Nédellec and Céline Rouveirol, editors, *Proceedings of the European Conference on Machine Learning (ECML)*, Berlin, Germany, 1998. Springer.
7. Thorsten Joachims. Transductive inference for text classification using support vector machines. In *Proceedings of the Sixteenth International Conference on Machine Learning (ICML-99)*, Bled, Slovenia, 1999.
8. Thorsten Joachims. Estimating the generalization performance of a SVM efficiently. In Pat Langley, editor, *Proceedings of the Seventeenth International Conference on Machine Learning (ICML-2000)*, pages 431–438, San Francisco, CA, USA, 2000. Morgan Kaufmann.
9. Thorsten Joachims. *The Maximum-Margin Approach to Learning Text Classifiers: Methods, Theory, and Algorithms*. PhD thesis, Computer Science Department, University of Dortmund, Germany, 2001.
10. Ralf Klinkenberg. Maschinelle Lernverfahren zum adaptiven Informationsfiltern bei sich verändernden Konzepten. Masters thesis, Computer Science Department, University of Dortmund, Germany, February 1998.
11. Ralf Klinkenberg. Using labeled and unlabeled data to learn drifting concepts. In Miroslav Kubat and Katharina Morik, editors, *Workshop notes of the IJCAI-01 Workshop on* Learning from Temporal and Spatial Data, pages 16–24, Menlo Park, CA, USA, 2001. AAAI Press. Held in conjunction with the International Joint Conference on Artificial Intelligence (IJCAI).
12. Ralf Klinkenberg and Thorsten Joachims. Detecting concept drift with support vector machines. In Pat Langley, editor, *Proceedings of the Seventeenth International Conference on Machine Learning (ICML)*, pages 487–494, San Francisco, CA, USA, 2000. Morgan Kaufmann.
13. Ralf Klinkenberg and Ingrid Renz. Adaptive information filtering: Learning in the presence of concept drifts. In Mehran Sahami, Mark Craven, Thorsten Joachims, and Andrew McCallum, editors, *Workshop Notes of the ICML/AAAI-98 Workshop on* Learning for Text Categorization *held at the* Fifteenth International Conference on Machine Learning *(ICML-98)*, pages 33–40, Menlo Park, CA, USA, 1998. AAAI Press.
14. A. Kuh, T. Petsche, and R. L. Rivest. Learning time-varying concepts. In *Advances in Neural Information Processing Systems*, volume 3, pages 183–189, San Mateo, CA, USA, 1991. Morgan Kaufmann.
15. Gerhard Kunisch. Anpassung und Evaluierung statistischer Lernverfahren zur Behandlung dynamischer Aspekte in Data Mining. Masters thesis, Computer Science Department, University of Ulm, Germany, June 1996.
16. Carsten Lanquillon. Dynamic neural classification. Masters thesis, Computer Science Department, University of Braunschweig, Germany, October 1997.

17. Carsten Lanquillon. Information filtering in changing domains. In Thorsten Joachims, Andrew McCallum, Mehran Sahami, and Lyle Ungar, editors, *Working Notes of the IJCAI-99 Workshop on* Machine Learning for Information Filtering *held at the* Sixteenth International Joint Conference on Artificial Intelligence, pages 41–48, Stockholm, Sweden, August 1999.

18. Carsten Lanquillon. Partially Supervised Text Classification: Combining Labeled and Unlabeled Documents Using an EM-like Scheme. In Ramon López de Mántaras and Enric Plaza, editors, *Proceedings of the 11th Conference on Machine Learning (ECML 2000)*, volume 1810 of *LNCS*, pages 229–237. Springer, Berlin, Germany, 2000.

19. Tom Mitchell, Rich Caruana, Dayne Freitag, John McDermott, and David Zabowski. Experience with a learning personal assistant. *Communications of the ACM*, 37(7):81–91, July 1994.

20. Kamal Nigam, Andrew McCallum, Sebastian Thrun, and Tom Mitchell. Learning to classify text from labeled and unlabeled documents. In Jack Mostow and Charles Rich, editors, *Proceedings of the Fifteenth National Conference on Artificial Intelligence (AAAI-98)*, pages 792–799, Menlo Park, CA, USA, 1998. AAAI Press /MIT Press.

21. Kamal Nigam, Andrew McCallum, Sebastian Thrun, and Tom Mitchell. Text Classification from Labeled and Unlabeled Documents using EM. *Machine Learning*, 39(2/3):103–134, 2000.

22. Oliver Ritthoff, Ralf Klinkenberg, Simon Fischer, Ingo Mierswa, and Sven Felske. YALE: Yet Another Machine Learning Environment. In R. Klinkenberg, S. Rüping, A. Fick, N. Henze, C. Herzog, R. Molitor, and O. Schröder, editors, *LLWA 01 – Tagungsband der GI-Workshop-Woche Lernen – Lehren – Wissen – Adaptivität*, pages 84–92, Technical Report No. 763, Department of Computer Science, University of Dortmund, October 2001. *http://yale.cs.uni-dortmund.de/*.

23. Stefan Rüping. *mySVM-Manual*. Artificial Intelligence Unit, Department of Computer Science, University of Dortmund, Germany, 2000. *http://www-ai.cs.uni-dortmund.de/SOFTWARE/MYSVM/*.

24. G. Salton and C. Buckley. Term weighting approaches in automatic text retrieval. *Information Processing and Management*, 24(5):513–523, 1988.

25. A. Smola, B. Schölkopf, and K.-R. Müller. General cost functions for support vector regression. In L. Niklasson, M. Boden, and T. Ziemke, editors, *Proceedings of the 8th International Conference on Artificial Neural Networks*, 1998.

26. Nadeem Ahmed Syed, Huan Liu, and Kah Kay Sung. Handling concept drifts in incremental learning with support vector machines. In *Proceedings of the Fifth International Conference on Knowledge Discovery and Data Mining*, New York, NY, USA, 1999. ACM Press.

27. Charles Taylor, Gholamreza Nakhaeizadeh, and Carsten Lanquillon. Structural change and classification. In G. Nakhaeizadeh, I. Bruha, and C. Taylor, editors, *Workshop Notes of the ECML-97 Workshop on* Dynamically Changing Domains: Theory Revision and Context Dependence Issues *held at the* Ninth European Conference on Machine Learning, pages 67–78, April 1997.

28. C. van Rijsbergen. A theoretical basis for the use of co-occurrence data in information retrieval. *Journal of Documentation*, 33(2):106–119, June 1977.

29. Vladimir Vapnik. *Statistical Learning Theory*. Wiley, Chichester, GB, 1998.

30. Gerhard Widmer and Miroslav Kubat. Learning in the presence of concept drift and hidden contexts. *Machine Learning*, 23(2):69–101, 1996.

Evaluating Retrieval Performance Using Clickthrough Data

Thorsten Joachims

Cornell University, Department of Computer Science,
Ithaca, NY 14853 USA,
tj@cs.cornell.edu

Abstract. This paper proposes a new method for evaluating the quality of retrieval functions. Unlike traditional methods that require relevance judgments by experts or explicit user feedback, it is based entirely on clickthrough data. This is a key advantage, since clickthrough data can be collected at very low cost and without overhead for the user. The paper proposes an experiment setup that generates unbiased feedback about the relative quality of two search results without explicit user feedback. A theoretical analysis shows that the method gives the same results as evaluation with traditional relevance judgments under mild assumptions. According to a small-scale empirical study, the assumptions appear justified and the new method leads to conclusive results in a WWW retrieval setting.

1 Introduction

User feedback can provide valuable information for analyzing and optimizing the performance of information retrieval systems. Unfortunately, experience shows that users are only rarely willing to give explicit feedback (e. g. [9]). To overcome this problem, this paper explores an approach to extracting information from implicit feedback. The user is not required to answer questions, but the system observes the user's behavior and infers implicit preference information automatically.

The particular retrieval setting studied in this paper is web search engines. In this setting, it seems out of question to ask users for relevance judgments about the documents returned. However, it is easy to observe the links the user clicked on. With search engines that receive millions of queries per day, the available quantity of such clickthrough data is virtually unlimited. This paper shows how it is possible to tap this information source to compare different search engines according to their effectiveness. The approach is based on the idea of designing a series of experiments (i.e. blind tests) for which clickthrough data provides an unbiased assessment under plausible assumptions.

2 Previous Work

Most evaluation in information retrieval is based on precision and recall using manual relevance judgments by experts [1]. However, especially for large and dynamic document collections, it becomes intractable to get accurate recall estimates, since they require relevance judgments for the full document collection. To some extend, focused sampling like in the pooling method [10] as used in TREC [21] can reduce assessment cost. The idea is to focus manual assessment on the top documents from several retrieval systems, since those are likely to contain most relevant documents. While some attempts have been made to evaluate retrieval functions without any human judgments using only statistics about the document collection itself [20][7][13], such evaluation schemes can only give approximate solutions and may fail to capture the users' preferences.

Retrieval systems for the WWW are typically not evaluated using recall. Instead, only their precision at N is measured [11][6]. This does not only decrease the amount of manual relevance assessment, but also – like the method presented in this paper – focuses the evaluation on those documents actually observed by the user [19]. However, the need for manual relevance judgments by experts still limits the scale and the frequency of evaluations.

The usefulness measure of Frei and Schäuble [4] uses a different form of human relevance assessment. With respect to being a relative performance criterion, it is similar to the method proposed in this paper. The usefulness measure is designed to compare two retrieval strategies without absolute relevance judgments. Referring to empirical studies [17][12], Frei and Schäuble argue that humans are more consistent at giving relative relevance statements. Furthermore, they recognize that relevance assessments are user and context dependent, so that relevance judgments by experts are not necessarily a good standard to compare against. Therefore, their method relies on relative preference statements from users. Given two sets of retrieved documents for the same query, the user is asked to judge the relative usefulness for all/some pairs of documents. These user preferences are then compared against the orderings imposed by the two retrieval functions and the respective number of violation is used as a score. While this technique eliminates the need for relevance judgments on the whole document collection, it still relies on manual relevance feedback from the user.

Some attempts have been made towards using implicit feedback by observing clicking behavior. For example, the search engine DirectHit uses clickthrough as a measure of popularity. Other search engines appear to record clickthrough, but do not state what use they make of it. Published results on using clickthrough data exist for experimental retrieval systems [3] and browsing assistants [14]. However, the semantics of such data is unclear as argued in the following.

3   Presentation Bias in Clickthrough Data

Which search engine provides better results: Google or MSNSearch? Evaluating such hypotheses is a problem of statistical inference. Unfortunately,

↓ f used for presentation	f used for evaluation		
	bxx	tfc	hand-tuned
bxx	**6.26**± 1.14	46.94±9.80	28.87± 7.39
tfc	54.02±10.63	**6.18**±1.33	13.76± 3.33
hand-tuned	48.52± 6.32	24.61±4.65	**6.04**± 0.92

Table 1. Average clickrank for three retrieval functions ("bxx" (no weighting [18]), "tfc" (TFIDF-cosine [18]), and a "hand-tuned" (TFIDF-cosine with different weights according to HTML tags) implemented in LASER. Rows correspond to the retrieval method used by LASER at query time; columns hold values from subsequent evaluation with other methods. Figures reported are means and two standard errors. This table is taken from [3].

regular clickthrough data is not suited to answer this question in a principled way. Consider the following setup:

Experiment Setup 1 (REGULAR CLICKTHROUGH DATA)
The user types a query into a unified interface and the query is sent to both search engines A and B. One of the returned rankings is selected at random and it is presented to the user. The ranks of the links the user clicked on are recorded.

An example of an observation from this experiment is the following: the user types in the query "support vector machine", receives the ranking from search enging B, and then clicks on the links ranked 1, 5, and 6. Data collected by Boyan et al. shows that this setup leads to a strong "presentation bias" [3], making the results difficult to interpret. Consider the average rank of the clicks as a performance measure (e.g. 4 in the example). What can one conclude from this type of clickthrough data?

Table 1 shows the average clickrank for three retrieval strategies averaged over ≈ 1400 queries. Rows correspond to the retrieval method presented to the user, while columns show the average clickrank from subsequent evaluation with all retrieval functions. Looking at the diagonal of the table, the average clickrank is almost equal for all methods. However, according to subjective judgments, the three retrieval functions are substantially different in their ranking quality. "Hand-tuned" is clearly the best, followed by "tfc", and "bxx" is very bad. The lack of difference in the observed average clickrank can be explained as follows. Since users typically scan only the first l (e.g. $l \approx 10$ [19]) links of the ranking, clicking on a link cannot be interpreted as a relevance judgment on an *absolute* scale. Maybe a document ranked much lower in the list was much more relevant, but the user never saw it. It appears that users click on the *relatively* most promising links in the top l, independent of their absolute relevance. This hypothesis is supported by the off-diagonal entries of Table 1, for which the clickrank evaluation is done on a ranking different from the one used for presentation. In all cases (i.e. rows), the average clickrank is lower for the subjectively better ranking method. Under the hypothesis that users click on the relatively best links in the top l of the presented ranking and that the subjective judgement of the three ranking methods is correct, this result is to be expected. However, it is difficult to derive a formal interpretation of this type of data.

Other statistics, like the number of links the user clicked on, are difficult to interpret as well. It is not clear if more clicks indicate a better ranking (i.e. the user found more relevant documents) or a worse ranking (i.e. the user had to look at more documents to fulfill the information need). These problems lead to the conclusion that Experiment Setup 1 leads to clickthrough data that is difficult to analyze in a principled way.

4   Unbiased Clickthrough Data for Comparing Retrieval Functions

While the previous experiment setup leads to biased data, we are free to design other forms of presentation that do not exhibit this property. In this light, designing the user interface becomes a question of experiment design. What are the criteria a user interface should fulfill so that clickthrough data is useful?

Blind Test: The interface should hide the random variables underlying the hypothesis test to avoid biasing the user's response. Like patients in medical trials, the user should not know, which one is the "drug" or the "placebo".

Click $\Rightarrow$ Preference: The interface should be designed so that a click during a natural interaction with the system demonstrates a particular judgment of the user.

Low Usability Impact: The interface should not substantially lower the productivity of the user. The system should still be useful, so that users are not turned away.

While Experiment Setup 1 is a blind test, it is not clear how clickthrough is connected to performance. Furthermore, this experiment can have considerable impact on the productivity of the user, since every second query is answered by an inferior retrieval strategy.

4.1   An Experiment Setup for Eliciting Unbiased Data

The following is a more suitable setup for deciding from clickthrough data whether one retrieval strategy is better than another. Under mild assumptions, it generates unbiased data for a hypothesis test from paired observations.

```
┌─────────────────────────────────────┐ ┌─────────────────────────────────────┐
│ Google Results:                       │ │ MSNSearch Results:                    │
│ 1. Kernel Machines                    │ │ 1. Kernel Machines                    │
│    http : //svm.first.gmd.de/         │ │    http : //svm.first.gmd.de/         │
│ 2. SVM-Light Support Vector Machine   │ │ 2. Support Vector Machine             │
│    http : //ais.gmd.de/.../svm_light/ │ │    http : //jbolivar.freeservers.com/ │
│ 3. Support Vector Machine ... References│ │ 3. An Introduction to Support Vector Machines│
│    http : //svm.....com/SVMrefs.html  │ │    http : //www.support − vector.net/ │
│ 4. Lucent Technologies: SVM demo applet│ │ 4. Archives of SUPPORT-VECTOR- ...    │
│    http : //svm.....com/SVT/SVMsvt.html│ │    http : //www.jiscmail.ac.uk/lists/...│
│ 5. Royal Holloway Support Vector Machine│ │ 5. SVM-Light Support Vector Machine  │
│    http : //svm.dcs.rhbnc.ac.uk/      │ │    http : //ais.gmd.de/.../svm_light/ │
│ 6. Support Vector Machine - The Software│ │ 6. Support Vector Machine - The Software│
│    http: //wwwsupport−vector.net/softwarehtml│ │    http: //wwwsupport−vector.net/softwarehtml│
│ 7. Support Vector Machine - Tutorial  │ │ 7. Lagrangian Support Vector Machine Home Page│
│    http: //wwwsupport−vector.net/tutorialhtml│ │    http: //www.cs.wisc.edu/dmi/lsvm  │
│ 8. Support Vector Machine             │ │ 8. A Support ... - Bennett, Blue (ResearchIndex)│
│    http : //jbolivar.freeservers.com/ │ │    http : //citeseer.../bennett97support.html│
└─────────────────────────────────────┘ └─────────────────────────────────────┘

┌─────────────────────────────────────┐
│ Combined Results:                     │
│ 1. Kernel Machines                    │
│    http : //svm.first.gmd.de/         │
│ 2. Support Vector Machine             │
│    http : //jbolivar.freeservers.com/ │
│ 3. SVM-Light Support Vector Machine   │
│    http : //ais.gmd.de/ ∼ thorsten/svm_light/│
│ 4. An Introduction to Support Vector Machines│
│    http : //www.support − vector.net/ │
│ 5. Support Vector Machine and Kernel Methods References│
│    http : //svm.research.bell − labs.com/SVMrefs.html│
│ 6. Archives of SUPPORT-VECTOR-MACHINES@JISCMAIL.AC.UK│
│    http : //www.jiscmail.ac.uk/lists/SUPPORT−VECTOR−MACHINES.html│
│ 7. Lucent Technologies: SVM demo applet│
│    http : //svm.research.bell − labs.com/SVT/SVMsvt.html│
│ 8. Royal Holloway Support Vector Machine│
│    http : //svm.dcs.rhbnc.ac.uk/      │
│ 9. Support Vector Machine - The Software│
│    http : //www.support − vector.net/software.html│
│ 10. Lagrangian Support Vector Machine Home Page│
│    http : //www.cs.wisc.edu/dmi/lsvm  │
└─────────────────────────────────────┘
```

Fig. 1. Example for query "support vector machine". The two upper boxes show the rankings returned by Google and MSNSearch. The lower box contains the combined ranking presented to the user. The links the user clicked on are marked in bold.

Experiment Setup 2 (UNBIASED CLICKTHROUGH DATA)
The user types a query into a unified interface. The query is sent to both search engines A and B. The returned rankings are mixed so that at any point the top l links of the combined ranking contain the top k_a and k_b links from rankings A and B, $|k_a - k_b| \leq 1$. The combined ranking is presented to the user and the ranks of the links the user clicked on are recorded.

Section 4.2 shows that such a combined ranking always exists. An example is given in Figure 1. The results of two search engines are combined into one ranking that is presented to the user. Note that the abstracts and all other aspects of the presentation are unified, so that the user cannot tell which retrieval strategy proposed a particular page. In the example, the user clicks on links 1, 3, and 7. What inference can one draw from these clicks?

Before going into a detailed statistical analysis in Section 5, let's first analyze this kind of data on an intuitive basis. If one assumes that a user scans the combined ranking from top to bottom without skipping links, this setup ensures that at any point during the scan the user has observed as many (± 1) links from the top of ranking A as from ranking B. In this way, the combined ranking gives (almost) equal presentation bias to both search engines. If one further assumes that the user is more likely to click on a more relevant link, and that the abstract provides enough information to judge relevance better than random, then the clicks convey information about the relative quality of the top $k_a \approx k_b$ links from both retrieval strategies. If the user clicks more often on links from retrieval strategy A, it is reasonable to conclude that the top $k_a \approx k_b$ links from A are more relevant than those from B. In the example from Figure 1 the user must have seen the top 4 links from both individual rankings, since he clicked on link 7 in the combined ranking. He decided to click on 3 links in the top 4 returned by Google (namely 1, 2, and 4), but only on 1 link from MSNSearch (namely 1). It is reasonable to conclude, that (with probability larger than random) the top 4 links from Google were judged to be better than those from MSNSearch for this query. A detailed analysis of the statistical properties of this type of data is subject to Section 5.

Summarizing Experiment Setup 2, it is a blind test in which clicks demonstrate the relative user preference in an unbiased way. Furthermore, the usability impact is low. In the worst case the user needs to scan twice as many links as for the better individual ranking. But the user is never stuck with just the worse retrieval strategy.

Before analyzing the statistical properties of the data generated in Experiment Setup 2, let's first consider the question of how a combined ranking can be constructed.

4.2   Computing the Combined Ranking

An algorithm for generating a combined ranking according to Experiment Setup 2 is the following.

Algorithm 1 (Combine Rankings)

Input: ranking $A = (a_1, a_2, \ldots)$, ranking $B = (b_1, b_2, \ldots)$
Call: combine(A,B,0,0,$\emptyset$)
Output: combined ranking D
combine(A,B,k_a,k_b,D) {
    if($k_a = k_b$) {
        if(A $[k_a + 1] \notin$ D) { D := D + A $[k_a + 1]$; }
        combine(A,B,$k_a + 1$,k_b,D);
    }
    else {
        if(B $[k_b + 1] \notin$ D) { D := D + B $[k_b + 1]$; }
        combine(A,B,k_a,$k_b + 1$,D);
    }
}

The following theorem shows that the algorithm always constructs a combined ranking with the desired property, even if there are duplicates between the two rankings.

Theorem 1. *Algorithm 1 always produces a combined ranking in the form* $D = (d_1, d_2, \ldots)$ *from* $A = (a_1, a_2, \ldots)$ *and* $B = (b_1, b_2, \ldots)$ *so that for all* n

$$\{d_1, \ldots, d_n\} = \{a_1, \ldots, a_{k_a}\} \cup \{b_1, \ldots, b_{k_b}\} \tag{1}$$

with $k_b \leq k_a \leq k_b + 1$.

Proof. Induction over the recursion depth.

Assumption: combine(A,B,k_a,k_b,D) has already constructed a mixed ranking with $\{d_1, \ldots, d_{n_d}\} = \{a_1, \ldots, a_{k_a}\} \cup \{b_1, \ldots, b_{k_b}\}$ and $k_b \leq k_a \leq k_b + 1$.
Start: Clearly this is true for the initial call combine(A,B,0,0,()).
Step: Given that the assumption is true, there are four cases to consider in the current iteration:

 Case $k_a = k_b$ and $A[k_a + 1] \notin D$: Then $A[k_a + 1]$ is appended to D and it holds that $\{d_1, \ldots, d_{n_d}, d_{n_d+1}\} = \{a_1, \ldots, a_{k_a}, a_{k_a+1}\} \cup \{b_1, \ldots, b_{k_b}\}$ and $k_a = k_b + 1$.
 Case $k_a = k_b$ and $A[k_a + 1] \in D$: Then $A[k_a + 1]$ is already in D so that $\{d_1, \ldots, d_{n_d}\} = \{a_1, \ldots, a_{k_a}, a_{k_a+1}\} \cup \{b_1, \ldots, b_{k_b}\}$ and $k_a = k_b + 1$.
 Case $k_a > k_b$ and $B[k_b + 1] \notin D$: Then $B[k_b + 1]$ is appended to D and it holds that $\{d_1, \ldots, d_{n_d}, d_{n_d+1}\} = \{a_1, \ldots, a_{k_a}\} \cup \{b_1, \ldots, b_{k_b}, b_{k_b+1}\}$ and $k_b = k_a$, since $k_a - k_b \leq 1$ by induction.
 Case $k_a > k_b$ and $B[k_b + 1] \in D$: Then $B[k_b + 1]$ is already in D so that $\{d_1, \ldots, d_{n_d}\} = \{a_1, \ldots, a_{k_a}\} \cup \{b_1, \ldots, b_{k_b}, b_{k_b+1}\}$ and $k_b = k_a$, since $k_a - k_b \leq 1$ by induction.

Note that Algorithm 1 gives ranking A a slight presentation bias, since it starts the combined ranking with a link from A and adds a link from A, if k_a and k_b are equal. To avoid a systematic bias, the retrieval strategy to start (or continue) with is selected randomly.

For simplicity reasons, the following treats k_a and k_b as if they were always equal. This is a relatively weak assumption, since the difference between k_a and k_b should have mean 0 due to randomization.

5   Theoretical Analysis

This section analyzes the statistical properties of the clickthrough data generated according to Experiment Setup 2. It will show how, under mild assumptions, this data is sufficient for statistical inference regarding the quality of rankings.

5.1   Connecting Relevance and Clickthrough

Let's consider the standard model of relevance with only two relevance values. Each document is either relevant for a query and a user in a particular context, or not. The quality of a retrieval function is higher the more relevant and the less non-relevant links it retrieves.

For this binary relevance model, the user's clicking behavior with respect to the different retrieval functions can be described using the following model. Capital letters stand for random variables, while the corresponding non-capitalized letter stands for a realization of that random variable.

$$\Pr(C_a, C_b, C_r, C_n, R_a, N_a, R_b, N_b, R, N) \tag{2}$$

Denote with l the number of links the user observes in the combined ranking. Determined by l, let $k = k_a = k_b$ be the number of links the user observes from the tops of rankings A and B before stopping. Then C_a is the number of clicks on links in the top k of ranking A, while C_b is the number of clicks on links in the top k of ranking B. C_r (C_n) denotes the number of clicks on relevant (non-relevant) links. Note, that c_a plus c_b does not necessarily sum to $c_r + c_n$, since the same link can be in the top k of both retrieval functions. Similarly, R_a, N_a, R_b, and N_b are the numbers of relevant and non-relevant links in the top k of A and B respectively. R and N are the total number of relevant and non-relevant links in the top l of the combined ranking. Note that $r_a + n_a + r_b + n_b$ is not necessarily equal to $l = r + n$, since both retrieval functions may propose the same links.

Which variables in Equation (2) can be observed? Obviously, we can observe C_a and C_b, as well as the total number of clicks $C_r + C_n$. Furthermore, we can approximate l with the rank of the last link the user clicked on. This makes it possible to compute k. To be precise, let $D = (d_1, d_2, \ldots)$ be the combined ranking of $A = (a_1, a_2, \ldots)$ and $B = (b_1, b_2, \ldots)$. Furthermore, let $u_1, \ldots, u_f$ be the ranks in D of the links the user clicked on sorted by increasing rank. Then compute k as the minimum rank of c_{u_f} in A and B

$$k = min\left\{ i : d_{u_f} = a_i \text{ or } d_{u_f} = b_i \right\}. \tag{3}$$

Define $k = 0$ for queries without clicks. Furthermore, define C_a and C_b as

$$c_a = |\{u_i : d_{u_i} \in (a_1, \ldots, a_k)\}|, \tag{4}$$

$$c_b = |\{u_i : d_{u_i} \in (b_1, \ldots, b_k)\}|. \tag{5}$$

The central question is now: under which assumptions do these observed variables allow inference regarding the variables of key interest – namely the numbers of relevant links R_a and R_b retrieved by A and B respectively? Let's first state the assumption that users click more frequently on relevant links than on non-relevant links.

Assumption 1.   *Given a ranking in which the user encounters r relevant links and n non-relevant links before he stops browsing. Denote with c the* number of links the user clicks on, whereas c_r of these links are relevant and c_n are non-relevant. Further denote with r_a and r_b the number of relevant links in the top k of rankings A and B respectively. It holds that

$$\mathcal{E}\left(\frac{C_r}{R\,C}|r_a - r_b\right) - \mathcal{E}\left(\frac{C_n}{N\,C}|r_a - r_b\right) = \epsilon > 0 \tag{6}$$

for some $\epsilon > 0$ and all differences between r_a and r_b with non-zero probability. $\mathcal{E}(\cdot)$ denotes the expectation.

Intuitively, this assumption formalizes that users click on a relevant link more frequently than on a non-relevant link by a difference of ϵ. The smaller ϵ, the more does the user treat both relevant and non-relevant links the same. In particular, $\epsilon = 0$ if the user clicks on links uniformly at random.

In one respect, this assumption is very weak. It merely implies that users can judge the relevance of a document given its abstract better than random, and that they behave "rational" in the sense that they tend to explore relevant links more frequently. Empirical results indicate that good abstracts can help users identify relevant documents substantially better than random [15]. However, the amount of information an abstract conveys about the relevance of a document is likely to depend on the type of query (e.g. home-page finding vs. fact finding). The assumption also states that the ϵ is constant over all values of $r_a - r_b$. In how far this is true will be evaluated experimentally in Section 6.3.

Given Experiment Setup 2, the clicks on relevant and non-relevant links can be further split up with respect to the different retrieval functions. Let's denote by C_{ra} the number of clicks on relevant links from A and by C_{na} the number of clicks on non-relevant links from A. The analogous quantities for B are C_{rb} and C_{nb}. Controlling the way of presenting the combined ranking to the users, one can make sure that they cannot tell which search engine retrieved a particular link. In the experiment setup used in this study, the same layout and abstract generator were used to present links. So, it is reasonable to assume that the distribution of clicks is not biased towards one retrieval strategy unless there is a difference in the number of relevant links retrieved. This is formalized by the following assumption.

Assumption 2

$$\mathcal{E}(C_{a,r}|c_r, c_n, r_a, n_a, r_b, n_b, r, n) = c_r \frac{r_a}{r} \tag{7}$$

$$\mathcal{E}(C_{a,n}|c_r, c_n, r_a, n_a, r_b, n_b, r, n) = c_n \frac{n_a}{n} \tag{8}$$

$$\mathcal{E}(C_{b,r}|c_r, c_n, r_a, n_a, r_b, n_b, r, n) = c_r \frac{r_b}{r} \tag{9}$$

$$\mathcal{E}(C_{b,n}|c_r, c_n, r_a, n_a, r_b, n_b, r, n) = c_n \frac{n_b}{n} \tag{10}$$

Intuitively, the assumption states that the only reason for a user clicking on a particular link is due to the relevance of the link, but not due to other influence factors connected with a particular retrieval function. One model that will produce the expected values from above is the following. Among the r relevant links, the user clicks on links uniformly without dependence on the retrieval function. This can be modeled by the hypergeometric distribution, which will produce the expected values from above. Note that – as desired – the distribution is symmetric with respect to swapping the retrieval functions A and B.

With these assumptions, it is possible to prove the following theorem. Intuitively, the theorem states that under Experiment Setup 2, evaluating clickthrough will lead to the same result as evaluating relevance judgments.

Theorem 2. *In Experiment Setup 2 and under Assumption 1 and Assumption 2, A retrieves more relevant links than B iff the clickthrough for A is higher than clickthrough for B (and vice versa).*

$$\mathcal{E}(R_a) > \mathcal{E}(R_b) \Longleftrightarrow \mathcal{E}\left(\frac{C_a}{C}\right) > \mathcal{E}\left(\frac{C_b}{C}\right) \tag{11}$$

$$\mathcal{E}(R_a) < \mathcal{E}(R_b) \Longleftrightarrow \mathcal{E}\left(\frac{C_a}{C}\right) < \mathcal{E}\left(\frac{C_b}{C}\right) \tag{12}$$

Proof. Let's start with proving (11). Instead of comparing the expected values, it is equivalent to determine the sign of the expected difference as follows.

$$\mathcal{E}\left(\frac{C_a}{C}\right) > E\left(\frac{C_b}{C}\right) \tag{13}$$

$$\Leftrightarrow \mathcal{E}\left(\frac{C_a - C_b}{C}\right) \geq 0 \tag{14}$$

Using that the number of clicks c equals the sum of c_r and c_n, the expected difference can be decomposed.

$$\mathcal{E}\left(\frac{C_a - C_b}{C}\right)$$

$$= \sum \mathcal{E}\left(\frac{C_a - C_b}{c_r + c_n} | c_r, c_n, r_a, n_a, r_b, n_b, r, n\right) \Pr(c_r, c_n, r_a, n_a, r_b, n_b, r, n)$$

$$= \sum \mathcal{E}\left(\frac{(C_{a,r} + C_{a,n}) - (C_{b,r} + C_{b_n})}{c_r + c_n} | c_r, c_n, r_a, n_a, r_b, n_b, r, n\right) \Pr(...)$$

$C_{a,r}$ $(C_{a,n})$ denotes the number of clicks on relevant (non-relevant) links from A. The respective numbers for ranking B are $C_{b,r}$ and $C_{b,n}$. Under Assumption 2 it is possible to replace $\mathcal{E}\left(\frac{(C_{a,r} + C_{a,n}) - (C_{b,r} + C_{b_n})}{c_r + c_n} | c_r, c_n, r_a, n_a, r_b, n_b, r, n\right)$

with a closed form expression.

$$\sum \mathcal{E}\left(\frac{(C_{a,r}+C_{a,n})-(C_{b,r}+C_{b_n})}{c_r+c_n}\Big| c_r, c_n, r_a, n_a, r_b, n_b, r, n\right) \Pr(c_r, c_n, r_a, n_a, r_b, n_b, r, n)$$

$$= \sum \frac{1}{c_r+c_n}\left((c_r\frac{r_a}{r}+c_n\frac{n_a}{n})-(c_r\frac{r_b}{r}+c_n\frac{n_b}{n})\right)\Pr(c_r, c_n, r_a, n_a, r_b, n_b, r, n)$$

$$= \sum \frac{1}{c}\left(c_r\frac{r_a-r_b}{r}+c_n\frac{n_a-n_b}{n}\right)\Pr(c_r, c_n, r_a, n_a, r_b, n_b, r, n)$$

$$= \sum \frac{1}{c}\left(c_r\frac{r_a-r_b}{r}+c_n\frac{(k-r_a)-(k-r_b)}{n}\right)\Pr(c_r, c_n, r_a, n_a, r_b, n_b, r, n)$$

$$= \sum (r_a-r_b)\left(\frac{c_r}{r\,c}-\frac{c_n}{n\,c}\right)\Pr(c_r, c_n, r_a, n_a, r_b, n_b, r, n)$$

$$= \sum (r_a-r_b)\mathcal{E}\left(\frac{C_r}{R\,C}-\frac{C_n}{N\,C}\Big| r_a-r_b\right)\Pr(r_a-r_b)$$

Using Assumption 1, the expectation $\mathcal{E}\left(\frac{C_r}{R C}-\frac{C_n}{N C}\big| r_a-r_b\right)$ is positive and constant, so that it does not influence the following inequality.

$$\sum (r_a-r_b)\mathcal{E}\left(\frac{C_r}{R C}-\frac{C_n}{N C}\Big| r_a-r_b\right)\Pr(r_a-r_b)\geq 0 \tag{15}$$

$$\Leftrightarrow \sum (r_a-r_b)\Pr(r_a-r_b)\geq 0 \tag{16}$$

$$\Leftrightarrow \mathcal{E}(R_a-R_b)\geq 0 \tag{17}$$

$$\Leftrightarrow \mathcal{E}(R_a)\geq \mathcal{E}(R_b) \tag{18}$$

The proof of (12) is analogous.

5.2 Hypothesis Tests

The previous section showed that in order to detect a difference in the expected numbers $\mathcal{E}(R_a)$ and $\mathcal{E}(R_b)$ of relevant links in A and B, it is sufficient to prove that

$$\mathcal{E}\left(\frac{C_a-C_b}{C}\right) \tag{19}$$

is different from zero. Given n paired observations $<\frac{c_{a,i}}{c_i},\frac{c_{b,i}}{c_i}>$, this question can be addressed using a two-tailed paired t-test (see e.g. [16]). It assumes that the difference $X:=\frac{C_a}{C}-\frac{C_b}{C}$ is distributed according to a normal distribution. The H_0 hypothesis is that X has zero mean. The t-test rejects H_0 at a significance level of 95%, if

$$\hat{x}\notin \left[-t_{n-1,97.5}\frac{\hat{\sigma}}{\sqrt{n}}, t_{n-1,97.5}\frac{\hat{\sigma}}{\sqrt{n}}\right] \tag{20}$$

where n is the sample size, $\hat{x}=\frac{1}{n}\sum(\frac{c_{a,i}}{c_i}-\frac{c_{b,i}}{c_i})$ is the sample mean, $\hat{\sigma}^2=\frac{1}{n-1}\sum(\frac{c_{a,i}}{c_i}-\frac{c_{b,i}}{c_i}-\hat{x})^2$ is the sample variance, and $t_{n-1,97.5}$ is the 97.5% quantile point of the t-distribution with $n-1$ degrees of freedom.

In practice, it is difficult to ensure that the assumption of normal distribution holds for small samples. To make sure that the results are not invalidated by an inappropriate parametric test, let's also consider a nonparametric test. Instead of a testing the mean, such tests typically consider the median. In our case, I will use a binomial sign test (i.e. McNemar's test) (see e.g. [16]) to detect a significant deviation of the median

$$\mathcal{M}\left(\frac{C_a - C_b}{C}\right) \tag{21}$$

from zero. Other test like the Wilcoxon rank test are more powerful, but the binomial sign test requires the least assumptions. The binomial sign test counts how often the difference $\frac{c_a}{c} - \frac{c_b}{c}$ is negative and positive. Let the number of negative differences be d_n and the number of positive differences be d_p. If the distribution has zero median, these variables are binomially distributed with parameter $p = 0.5$. The test rejects the H_0 hypothesis of zero median with confidence greater 95%, if

$$2 \sum_{i=0}^{min\{d_p,d_n\}} \binom{d_n + d_p}{i} 0.5^{d_n+d_p} < 0.05 \tag{22}$$

Note that the median equals the mean for symmetric distributions. Therefore a significant result from a binomial sign test implies a significant difference of the mean under the Gaussian assumption.

In the following empirical evaluation both the t-test and the binomial sign test will be used in parallel.

6   Experiments

To evaluate the method proposed in this paper, it was applied to pairwise comparisons between Google, MSNSearch, and a default strategy. The default strategy is added as a baseline retrieval strategy and consists of the 50 (or less, if fewer hits were returned) links from MSNSearch in reverse order. One can expect that the default strategy performs substantially worse than both Google and MSNSearch.

6.1   Data

The data was gathered from three users (including myself) during the 25th of September and the 18th of October, 2001, using a simple proxy system. The user types the query into a search form which connects to a CGI script. The script selects two search engines in a randomized way, queries the individual search engines, and composes the combined ranking. For each link the URL and the title of the page are presented to the user. The user does not get any clues about which search engine is responsible for which link in the combined ranking. Each click of the user is routed through a proxy that records the action and uses the HTTP-Location command to forward to the desired page.

Over all, 180 queries and 211 clicks were recorded. The average number of clicks per query is 1.17. Among these are 39 queries without clicks. The average number of words per query is 2.31. This is comparable to the findings in [19] who report 2.35 words per query for an AltaVista query log. Reflecting the distribution of WWW usage by researchers in computer science, many of the queries were for personal home pages and known items. For such queries the title and the URL provide a good summary for judging the relevance of a page.

For evaluating the method proposed in this paper, manual relevance judgments were collected for the whole dataset. For each of the 180 queries, the top k links of both retrieval strategies (with k as defined in Equation (3)) were judged according to binary relevance. Again, the judgments were performed in a blind fashion. When assigning relevance judgments it was not observable how any search engine ranked the link, and whether the user clicked on the link. In particular, the order in which the links were presented for relevance judgment was randomized to avoid systematic presentation bias. Overall, 180 links were judged to be relevant[1].

6.2   Does the Clickthrough Evaluation Agree with the Relevance Judgments?

Table 2 shows the clickthrough data. Column 3 and 4 indicate for how many queries the user clicked on more links from A or B respectively. According to the binomial sign test, the differences between Google and Default, as well as between MSNSearch and Default are significant. The difference between Google and MSNSearch has a p-value of around 90%. The t-test delivers a similar p-value. On average, 77% of the clicks per query were on links in the top k of Google vs. 63% on links in the top k of MSNSearch. For Google vs. Random (85% vs. 18%) and MSNSearch vs. Random (91% vs. 12%) the difference is again significant.

How does this result compare to an evaluation with manual relevance judgments? Table 3 has the same form as Table 2, but compares the number of links judged relevant instead of the number of clicks. The conclusions from the manual relevance judgments closely follow those from the clickthrough data. Again, the difference between Google and Default, as well as MSNSearch and Default is significant according to the binomial sign test. The difference between Google and MSNSearch achieves a p-value of approximately 80%.

For all three comparisons, the result from Theorem 2 holds. The average number of relevant links is higher for Google (0.81) than for MSNSearch

---

[1] The equality with the number of queries is coincidental. Note that these 180 are not all the existing relevant links, but merely those in the region of the ranking that was explored by the user. In particular, no links were manually judged for queries without clicks.

A	B	$c_a > c_b$ (A better)	$c_a < c_b$ (B better)	$c_a = c_b > 0$ (tie)	$c_a = c_b = 0$	total
Google	MSNSearch	34	20	46	23	123
Google	Default	18	1	3	12	34
MSNSearch	Default	17	2	1	4	24

Table 2. Comparison using pairwise clickthrough data. The counts indicate for how many queries a user clicked on more links in the top k of the respective search engine.

A	B	$r_a > r_b$ (A better)	$r_a < r_b$ (B better)	$r_a = r_b > 0$ (tie)	$r_a = r_b = 0$	total
Google	MSNSearch	26	17	51	29	123
Google	Default	19	1	1	13	34
MSNSearch	Default	15	1	0	8	24

Table 3. Comparison using manual relevance judgments. The counts indicate for how many queries there were more relevant links in the top k of the respective search engine.

(0.72) in their pairwise comparison. For Google vs. Random the averages are 0.65 vs. 0.09, and for MSNSearch vs. Random the averages are 0.71 vs. 0.04. This shows that the difference in clickthrough data from Experiment Setup 2 does not only predict whether one retrieval strategy is better than another, but that it also indicates the quantity of the difference.

While this validates that the model makes reasonable predictions, an analysis of the individual assumptions can provide further insight regarding its adequacy.

6.3   Is Assumption 1 Valid?

Assumption 1 states that the user clicks on more relevant links than non-relevant links on average. In particular, it states that the difference is independent of how many relevant links were suggested by retrieval strategy A compared to B. Given the relevance judgments, this assumption can be tested against data. Let I_d be the set of queries with $r_a - r_b = d$ and $d \neq 0$. Then Table 4 shows the quantity

$$\hat{\epsilon}_d = \frac{1}{I_d} \sum_{I_d} \frac{c_r}{c\,r} - \frac{1}{I_d} \sum_{I_d} \frac{c_n}{c\,n} \tag{23}$$

for the three pairwise comparisons. Only those averages are shown, for which there were more than 2 observations. The first observation is that the value of ϵ is substantially above 0. This means that, in fact, users click much more frequently on relevant links than on non-relevant links. Furthermore, the

| A | B | $R_a - R_b$ | |
		-1	+1
Google	MSNSearch	0.73 ± 0.11	0.71 ± 0.09
Google	Default	—	0.76 ± 0.08
MSNSearch	Default	—	0.85 ± 0.07

Table 4. The estimated value of ϵ from Assumption 1 depending on the difference $R_a - R_b$ with one standard error. Only such estimates are shown, for which there are more than two observations.

particular value of ϵ is rather stable independent of $r_a - r_b$. In particular, all values are within errorbars. While this does not prove the validity of the assumption, it does verify that it is not vastly invalid.

6.4   Is Assumption 2 Valid?

Assumption 2 states that users do not click more frequently on links from one retrieval strategy independent of the relevance of the links. While it would take orders of magnitude more data to verify Assumption 2 in detail, the following summary already provides an effective check. If Assumption 2 holds, then the following equalities hold.

$$\mathcal{E}(C_r \frac{R_a}{R}) = \mathcal{E}(C_{r,a}) \tag{24}$$

$$\mathcal{E}(C_r \frac{R_b}{R}) = \mathcal{E}(C_{r,b}) \tag{25}$$

$$\mathcal{E}(C_n \frac{N_a}{N}) = \mathcal{E}(C_{n,a}) \tag{26}$$

$$\mathcal{E}(C_n \frac{N_b}{N}) = \mathcal{E}(C_{n,b}) \tag{27}$$

Accordingly, Table 5 compares the expected number of clicks (i.e. left side of equations) with the observed number of clicks (right side of equations). In general, the equalities appear to hold for real data. Only the observed numbers of clicks on non-relevant links for the comparisons against the default strategy are slightly elevated. However, this is not necessarily an inherent problem of Assumption 2, but more likely a problem with the binary relevance scale. Such relevance judgments cannot model small differences in relevance. This becomes particularly obvious in the comparison of MSNSearch and Default (remember that Default is the top 50 links of MSNSearch in reverse). A link in the top 10 of MSNSearch is likely to be more relevant than one ranked 40-50, even if it is not strictly relevant. The slight user preference for "non-relevant" links from MSNSearch (and Google) is likely to be due to this unmeasured difference in relevance. So, this clicking behavior is desirable, since it is likely to be related to relevance in a more fine-grained relevance model.

A	B	C_{ra} exp obs	C_{rb} exp obs	C_{na} exp obs	C_{nb} exp obs
Google	MSNSearch	75.9 ≈ 78	67.8 ≈ 67	23.0 ≈ 26	22.8 ≈ 22
Google	Default	21.0 ≈ 21	3.0 ≈ 3	6.7 ≈ 10	8.9 ≈ 8
MSNSearch	Default	15.0 ≈ 15	1.0 ≈ 1	5.3 ≈ 9	5.4 ≈ 3

Table 5. Compares the expected (exp) number of clicks according to Assumption 2 with the observed (obs) number of clicks.

7   Conclusions and Future Work

This paper presented a new method for evaluating retrieval functions that does not require (expensive and slow) manual relevance judgments. Its key idea is to design the user interface so that the resulting (cheap and timely) clickthrough data conveys meaningful information about the relative quality of two retrieval functions. This makes it possible to evaluate retrieval performance more economically, without delay, and in a more user-centered way. As desired, the measure is likely to reflect the preferences of the users in their current context, not that of an expert giving relevance judgments, and it evaluates only that portion of the ranking observed by the user.

The paper introduces a theoretical model and shows under which assumptions clickthrough data will give the same results as an evaluation using optimal relevance judgments. The predictions of the new method, as well as the individual assumptions are evaluated against real data in a small-scale study. For the users considered in the experiment, the results of the evaluation using clickthrough data were found to closely follow the relevance judgments and the assumptions were found to be reasonable.

Open questions include in how far this method can be applied in other domains. In particular, it is not clear whether the method is equally effective also for other types of users with different search interests and behaviors. Furthermore, it should be possible to increase the effectiveness of the method by incorporate more informative forms of unintrusive feedback, like time spent on a page, scrolling behavior, etc.

Comparing a small set of hypotheses as considered in this paper is the most basic form of learning. The eventual goal of this research is to automatically learn retrieval functions. While previous such learning approaches [5,2] require explicit feedback data in form of relevance judgments, first results on exploiting clickthrough data for learning a ranking function from relative preference examples are available [8].

Acknowledgements

Many thanks to Katharina Morik and the AI unit at the University of Dortmund for providing their help and the resources for the experiments. Thanks also to Christin Schäfer, Norbert Fuhr, and Phoebe Sengers for helpful comments.

References

1. R. Baeza-Yates and B. Ribeiro-Neto. *Modern Information Retrieval.* Addison-Wesley-Longman, Harlow, UK, May 1999.
2. B. Bartell, G. Cottrell, and R. Belew. Automatic combination of multiple ranked retrieval systems. In *Annual ACM SIGIR Conf. on Research and Development in Information Retrieval (SIGIR)*, pages 173–181, 1994.
3. J. Boyan, D. Freitag, and T. Joachims. A machine learning architecture for optimizing web search engines. In *AAAI Workshop on Internet Based Information Systems*, pages 1 – 8, August 1996.
4. H. Frei and P. Schäuble. Determining the effectiveness of retrieval algorithms. *Information Processing and Management*, 27(2/3):153–164, 1991.
5. N. Fuhr. Optimum polynomial retrieval functions based on the probability ranking principle. *ACM Transactions on Information Systems*, 7(3):183–204, 1989.
6. M. Gordon and P. Pathak. Finding information on the world wide web: the retrieval effectiveness of search engines. *Information Processing and Management*, 35:141–180, 1999.
7. R. Jin, C. Falusos, and A. Hauptmann. Meta-scoring: Automatically evaluating term weighting schemes in ir without precision-recall. In *Annual ACM SIGIR Conf. on Research and Development in Information Retrieval (SIGIR01)*, pages 83–89, 2001.
8. T. Joachims. Optimizing search engines using clickthrough data. In *Proceedings of the ACM Conference on Knowledge Discovery and Data Mining (KDD)*, 2002.
9. T. Joachims, D. Freitag, and T. Mitchell. WebWatcher: a tour guide for the world wide web. In *Proceedings of International Joint Conference on Artificial Intelligence (IJCAI)*, volume 1, pages 770 – 777. Morgan Kaufmann, 1997.
10. K. S. Jones and C. van Rijsbergen. Report on the need for and provision of an "ideal" information retrieval test collection. British Library Research and Development Report 5266, University of Cambridge, Computer Laboratory, 1975.
11. H. Leighton and J. Srivastava. First 20 precision among world wide web search services. *Journal of the American Society for Information Science*, 50(10):870–881, 1999.
12. M. Lesk and G. Salton. Relevance assessments and retrieval system evaluation. *Information Storage and Retrieval*, 4(3):343–359, 1968.
13. L. Li and Y. Shang. A new method for automatic performance comparison of search engines. *World Wide Web*, 3:241–247, 2000.
14. H. Lieberman. Letizia: An agent that assists Web browsing. In *Proceedings of the Fifteenth International Joint Conference on Artificial Intelligence (IJCAI '95)*, pages 924–929, Montreal, Canada, 1995. Morgan Kaufmann.
15. I. Mani, D. House, G. Klein, L. Hirschman, T. Firmin, and B. Sundheim. The tipster summac text summarization evaluation. In *Conference of the European Chapter of the Association for Computational Linguistics (EACL)*, pages 77–85, 1999.

16. A. Mood, F. Graybill, and D. Boes. *Introduction to the Theory of Statistics.* McGraw-Hill, 3rd edition, 1974.
17. A. Rees and D. Schultz. A field experimental approach to the study of relevance assessments in relation to document searching. NSF Report, 1967.
18. G. Salton and C. Buckley. Term weighting approaches in automatic text retrieval. *Information Processing and Management,* 24(5):513–523, 1988.
19. C. Silverstein, M. Henzinger, H. Marais, and M. Moricz. Analysis of a very large altavista query log. Technical Report SRC 1998-014, Digital Systems Research Center, 1998.
20. I. Soboroff, C. Nicholas, and P. Cahan. Ranking retrieval systems without relevance judgements. In *Annual ACM SIGIR Conf. on Research and Development in Information Retrieval (SIGIR01),* pages 66–73, 2001.
21. E. Voorhees and D. Harman. Overview of the eighth text retrieval conference. In *The Eighth Text REtrieval Conference (TREC 8),* 1999.

Towards Collaborative Information Retrieval: Three Approaches

Armin Hust, Stefan Klink, Markus Junker, and Andreas Dengel

German Research Center for Artificial Intelligence (DFKI GmbH),
P.O. Box 2080, 67608 Kaiserslautern, Germany
{armin.hust, stefan.klink, markus.junker, andreas.dengel}@dfki.de

Abstract. The accuracy of ad-hoc document retrieval systems has plateaued in the last few years. At DFKI, we are working on so-called collaborative information retrieval (CIR) systems which unintrusively learn from their users' search processes. As a first step towards techniques, we focus on a restricted setting in CIR in which only old queries and correct answer documents to these queries are available for improving on a new query. For this restricted setting we propose three initial approaches, called QSD, QLD, and TCL as well as combinations of these approaches with pseudo relevance feedback. The approaches are evaluated experimentally on standard Information Retrieval test collections. It turns out that in particular the hybrid approaches with pseudo relevance feedback give promising results. A bigger advantage of the proposed approaches is expected in real word test scenarios in which the overlap of user interests is larger than in our experimental set up.

1 Introduction

Information Retrieval (IR) Systems have been studied in Computer Science for decades. The traditional ad-hoc task in Information Retrieval is to find all documents relevant for an ad-hoc given query. Much work has been done on improving this task, in particular in the Text Retrieval Evaluation Conference series (TREC) [10]. In 1998, it was decided at TREC-8 that this task should no longer be pursued within TREC, in particular because the accuracy has plateaued in the last few years. At DFKI, we are working on approaches for Collaborative Information Retrieval (CIR) which learn to improve retrieval effectiveness from the interaction of different users with the retrieval engine. Such systems may have the potential to overcome the current plateau in ad-hoc retrieval.

Figure 1 illustrates the general scenario of CIR. A document retrieval system is typically used by many users. A typical search in a retrieval system consists of several query formulations. Often, the answer documents to the first query do not directly satisfy the user. Instead, he has to reformulate his query taking the answer documents found into consideration. Such refinement may consist of specializations as well as generalizations of previous queries. In general, satisfying an information need requires to go through a search process with many decisions on query reformulations. The idea of CIR is to store these search processes as well as the ratings of documents returned by the system (if available) in an archive. Subsequent users with similar interests and queries should then benefit from knowledge automatically acquired by the CIR system based on the stored search processes. This should result in shorter search processes and better retrieval quality for subsequent users.

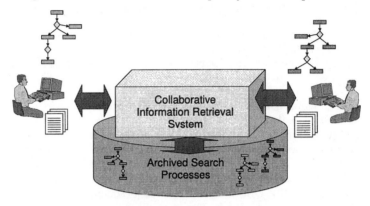

Fig. 1. Scenario of Collaborative Information Retrieval.

In this paper we focus on the investigation of a simple CIR scenario. Given a number of old queries posed by different users and their corresponding answer documents, we try to improve on an arbitrary new query.

In section 2 we first introduce the well-known vector space model and the formal description of the task we are tackling. The first two approaches described in section 3 both rely on measuring the similarity of a new query to former ones for which relevant documents are known. In section 4 we propose an approach which extends queries by extending the query terms individually. In section 5 we introduce pseudo relevance feedback and its combination with our three approaches. Section 6 describes the experimental setup using standard IR test collections and section 7 presents the results and compares them with the vector space model and the pseudo relevance feedback model. In section 8 we briefly review our new methods.

2   Basics and Terminology

In this section we briefly recall the vector space model for Information Retrieval on which all of our approaches rely (section 2.1). We then formalize the CIR scenario we are focussing on in this paper (section 2.2).

2.1   The Vector Space Model

The basic retrieval model we rely on is the vector space model (VSM)[1], [6]. In this model documents as well as queries are represented by vectors. The relevance of a document with respect to a query is mapped to a similarity function between the query vector and all document vectors. More formally, documents as well as queries are represented by vectors $(w_1, w_2, ..., w_n)$. Each position i in the vectors corresponds to a specific term w_i in the collection. The value w_i indicates the weighted presence or absence of the respective term in the document or query. For weighting we rely on a variant of the standard tf-idf weighting schema [1]. In this weighting schema a word is weighted higher in a document/query if it occurs more often in the document/query. It is also weighted higher if the word is rare in the document collection. The similarity sim between a given query q and a document d is computed by

$$sim(d, q) = \frac{d \cdot q}{\| d \| \cdot \| q \|} \qquad (1)$$

where $\| \cdot \|$ is the Euclidean norm of a vector. For retrieving all documents to a given query, all documents D of the underlying collection are ranked according to their similarity to the query and the top-ranked documents are given to the user.

2.2 Restricted CIR Scenario

As we have stated in the introduction, in this paper we focus on a restricted CIR scenario. In this scenario we have a set of old (former) queries $Q = \{q_1, \ldots, q_m\}$ available. For each $q \in Q$ the set of corresponding relevant documents is known and denoted by R_q. The goal now is to find all relevant documents for a new query $q^\star$ based on the old queries Q and their relevant documents $R_q, q \in Q$ (in general $q^\star \notin Q$). This is done by expanding the query $q^\star$ to a new query $q^\star_{\exp}$ which is then used instead of $q^\star$. More formally, let $\mathbf{Q}$ be queries and $\mathbf{D}$ documents. We are searching for an expansion function

$$
\begin{aligned}
f_{\exp} &: \mathbf{Q} \times 2^{(\mathbf{Q} \times (2^{\mathbf{D}}))} \to \mathbf{Q} \\
(q^\star, \{(q_1, R_{q_1}), (q_2, R_{q_2}), \ldots, (q_m, R_{q_m})\}) &\mapsto q^\star_{\exp}
\end{aligned} \qquad (2)
$$

which maximizes the effectiveness of $q^\star_{\exp}$.

3 Query Similarity-Based Approaches

The first two approaches presented in this section both rely on measuring the similarity between a new query and the old queries for which the answer documents are known.

3.1 QSD

The simple QSD approach (abbreviating "Query Similarity and relevant Documents") selects those former queries which are most similar to the new one. The relevant documents to each of these queries are represented by averaged document vectors. The expanded query is obtained by adding the weighted averaged document vectors to the original query.

The formal description is given here. The similarity $sim(q^\star, q)$ between the new query $q^\star$ and a query q is measured by the cosine of the angle between these two M dimensional vectors (cmp. equation 1):

$$sim(q^\star, q) = \frac{q^\star \cdot q}{\|q^\star\| \cdot \|q\|} \tag{3}$$

The set

$$Q_{q^\star} = \{q \in Q \mid sim(q, q^\star) \geq \vartheta\} \tag{4}$$

denotes all known queries which have a similarity to $q^\star$ greater than or equal to ϑ. The document vector r_q averages all documents which are relevant for query q:

$$r_q = \frac{\sum_{d \in R_q} d}{\|\sum_{d \in R_q} d\|} \tag{5}$$

Using $Q_{q^\star}$ and r_q, the expanded query vector $q^\star_{\text{exp}}$ is computed by:

$$q^\star_{\text{exp}} = q^\star + \sum_{q \in Q_{q^\star}} sim(q^\star, q) \cdot r_q \tag{6}$$

Thus, $q^\star_{\text{exp}}$ is the expansion by representatives of the answer documents to the queries most similar to $q^\star$. Note that the parameter of the QSD method is ϑ.

3.2 QLD

In general, a new query to be expanded by QSD consists of multiple words. The expansion depends on those former queries which have a high similarity to the new query. It can be that the high similarity of these most similar queries completely relies on just a subset of the terms in the original query. Thus, other terms of the new query will not be taken into account for the expansion. The QLD (Query Linear combination and relevant Documents) approach does not suffer from this potential drawback. It approximates the new query as a linear combination of similar former queries. The new query is then expanded by the answer documents to those queries which constitute the linear combination.

More formally, in the QLD approach a new query $q^\star$ is to be represented as a linear combination of the most similar former queries $Q_{q^\star} = \{q_1, q_2, \ldots, q_{m^\star}\}$:

$$q^\star = \sum_{i=1}^{m^\star} \lambda_i q_i \tag{7}$$

with λ_i being linear coefficients. In most cases we cannot represent the new query $q^\star$ exactly as a linear combination of the old queries $Q_{q^\star}$, i.e. equation 7 will have no solution. In order to solve this problem we write 7 as

$$q^\star = (q_1, q_2, \ldots, q_{m^\star}) \lambda \tag{8}$$

where $(q_1, q_2, \ldots, q_{m^\star})$ is a matrix with n rows and $m^\star$ columns and $\lambda = (\lambda_1, \lambda_2, \ldots, \lambda_{m^\star})$ is a column vector of dimension $m^\star$. In this situation we have to find a vector $\hat{\lambda}$ which provides the closest fit to the equation in some sense. Our approach is to minimize the Euclidean norm of the vector $(q_1, q_2, \ldots, q_{m^\star}) \lambda - q^\star$, i.e we solve

$$\hat{\lambda} = \mathrm{argmin}_\lambda \, \|(q_1, q_2, \ldots, q_{m^\star}) \lambda - q\| \tag{9}$$

with $\hat{\lambda} = (\hat{\lambda}_1, \hat{\lambda}_2, \ldots, \hat{\lambda}_{m^\star})$ being the least squares solution for the equation system.

For the expansion of the new query $q^\star$ only those queries $q_i \in Q_{q^\star}$ are taken into account which significantly contribute to the representation of $q^\star$, i.e., the corresponding $|\hat{\lambda}_i|$ must exceed some threshold $\vartheta_{\hat{\lambda}}$:

$$\tilde{\lambda}_i = \begin{cases} \hat{\lambda}_i \text{ if } |\hat{\lambda}_i| \geq \vartheta_{\hat{\lambda}} \\ 0 \text{ if } |\hat{\lambda}_i| < \vartheta_{\hat{\lambda}} \end{cases} \tag{10}$$

The expanded query $q^\star_{\mathrm{exp}}$ is obtained by adding the weighted representatives of the answer documents of those queries whose linear combination approximates the original query $q^\star$ best:

$$q^\star_{\mathrm{exp}} = q^\star + \sum_{q \in Q_{q^\star}} \tilde{\lambda}_q r_q \tag{11}$$

In addition to the parameter ϑ as in the QSD approach, the QLD approach has the parameter $\vartheta_{\hat{\lambda}}$.

4   Query Term-Based Approach

The two approaches QSD and QLD rely on measuring the similarity of a
new query and old queries with known answer documents. In this section we
present an approach which expands a query by expanding each query term
individually. The TCL (Term Concept Learning) approach learns concept
vectors for all terms that occur in former queries. These concepts are represented by concept vectors. They are computed by the documents relevant to
all former queries containing the respective term. For the expansion of a new
query, for each term in the query the corresponding concept vector is added.
More formally, the TCL approach uses the sets $Q_i \subset Q$ of all former queries
which contain the term with the index i:

$$Q_i = \{(w_1, ..., w_i, ..., w_n) \in Q \mid w_i \neq 0\} \tag{12}$$

The document set C_i denotes all documents relevant for at least one query
in Q_i, i.e., all documents which are relevant to at least one query containing
the term with index i:

$$C_i = \bigcup_{q \in Q_i} R_q \tag{13}$$

A representative concept vector for all documents contained in C_i is built by

$$c_i = \sum_{d \in C_i} d \tag{14}$$

The expansion $q^\star_{\mathrm{exp}}$ of the new query $q^\star = (w^\star_1, \ldots, w^\star_m)$ is now given by

$$q^\star_{\mathrm{exp}} = q^\star + \sum_{w^\star_i \neq 0} c_i \tag{15}$$

i.e., to all terms occurring in $q^\star$ the corresponding concept vector c_i is added.
In contrast to QSD and QLD, the TCL approach has no parameters.

5   Pseudo Relevance Feedback

Pseudo Relevance Feedback (PRF) is a well-known technique in the VSM. It
can improve the effectiveness of the original VSM approach as described in
section 2. We use it in two different ways. First, it is used as a stand-alone
retrieval technique (as described in section 5.1) for experimental comparisons.
Secondly, we combine it with our query expansion approaches QSD, QLD,
and TCL to new hybrid approaches. The combination and its motivation is
described in section 5.2.

5.1   Stand-Alone Technique

Pseudo relevance feedback (PRF) is a well-known query expansion technique [9,2]. In contrast to our approaches, it relies purely on the document collection and does not use former queries for expanding a new query. PRF enriches a new query q^* by the terms of the top-ranked documents with respect to q^*. We are using a variation of PRF as described in [5]. Let D_{q^*} be the set of document vectors given by

$$D_{q^*} = \left\{ d \in D \,\middle|\, \frac{sim(d, q^*)}{\max_{d' \in D}\{sim(d', q^*)\}} \geq \theta \right\} \tag{16}$$

where q^* is the original query and θ is a similarity threshold. The expanded query vector $q^*_{\exp}$ is obtained by

$$q^*_{\exp} = q^* + \alpha \frac{p}{\|p\|}, \text{ with } p = \sum_{d \in D_{q^*}} d \tag{17}$$

Note that the PRF approach has two parameters, θ and α.

5.2   Combination with New Approaches

We expect our approaches to be particulary useful if there is some overlap in the user queries. In contrast, PRF cannot exploit previous queries but just uses the document collection to be retrieved for query expansion. It is obvious that a combination of both approaches might be fruitful.

Our combination of PRF with QSD, QLD, and TCL is straight-forward. First, QSD/QLD/TCL is used to expand the query q^*. The expanded query q^*_{exp} is then expanded again by PRF as described above. We denote the combined approaches as PRF(QSD), PRF(QLD), and PRF(TCL).

6   Experimental Setup

We use standard Information Retrieval test collections for our experiments as provided by [8] and [10]. These collections were originally made for evaluating the effectiveness of different IR systems in a wide range of (artificial) queries. The collections offer the advantage that for all queries the correct answer documents are known. On the other hand the queries are very likely not typical for real world document retrieval systems. In particular, as opposed to real world systems, we expect little overlap in query topics. This may harm the performance of our approaches.

In the experiments we used three collections of the SMART system: "CACM" (titles and abstracts from the journal 'Communications of the "ACM"'), "CISI" (texts from the Institute of Scientific Information) and

CRAN ("Cranfield" collection, abstracts of Aerodynamics). The CR collection (congressional reports) of the TREC conference provides three different lengths for the queries from which we generated three test sets: "CR-title" contains the "title" queries (the shortest query representation), the "CR-desc" contains the "description" queries (the medium length query representation), the "CR-narr" contains the "narrative" queries (the longest query representation). Also from TREC we used the collection "FR" (federal register entries) and a modified version of the "AP90" collection. The questions in AP90 have one particularity: they were built by first defining 500 individual queries and then adding 193 reformulations to some of the original queries [11]. The modified version, which we call "AP90*" was generated by taking only the questions 201-893 which had at least one answer document in AP90 and only those documents of "AP90" which were relevant to at least one question. We thus resulted in 353 queries and 723 documents.

Table 1 lists some statistics about the collections we used after stemming and stop word elimination has been carried out.

Table 1. Statistics about test collections

	CACM	CISI	CRAN	CR-title	CR-desc	CR-narr	FR	AP90*
size(MB)	1.2	1.4	1.4	93	93	93	69	3.7
number of docs	3204	1460	1400	27922	27922	27922	19860	723
number of terms	3029	5755	2882	45717	45717	45717	50866	17502
mean doc length	18.4	38.2	49.8	188.2	188.2	188.2	189.7	201.8
	(short)	(med)	(med)	(long)	(long)	(long)	(long)	(long)
number of queries	52	112	225	34	34	34	112	353
mean query length	9.3	23.3	8.5	2.9	7.2	22.8	9.2	3.2
	(med)	(long)	(med)	(short)	(med)	(long)	(med)	(short)
mean num. of rel.	15.3	27.8	8.2	24.8	24.8	24.8	8.4	2.8
docs per query	(med)	(high)	(med)	(high)	(high)	(high)	(med)	(low)

The evaluation of the new learning methods (QSD, QLD, TCL, PRF(QSD), PRF(QLD), and PRF(TCL)) was done using a leave-one-out technique: From the set of queries $Q = \{q_1, \ldots q_n\}$ in a collection, we selected each $q_k \in Q$ and expanded it based on the queries $Q \setminus q_k$. Effectiveness was measured using macro-averaged recall/precision and averaged precision. Details on these measures can be found in [1]. In order to identify significant differences among methods we use the macro-averaged t-test (see, e.g., [12]) on the averaged precision.

7   Results

Some of the methods we compared contain parameters. For all methods with parameters we first searched for the parameter setting maximizing the average precision for a collection. The following parameters were tested:

- for PRF: $\alpha \in \{0, 0.1, \ldots, 2.0\}$ and $\theta \in \{0, 0.05, \ldots, 1.0\}$

- for QSD: $\vartheta \in \{0, 0.01, \ldots, 1.00\}$
- for QLD: $\vartheta \in \{0, 0.01, \ldots, 1.00\}$ and $\vartheta_{\hat{\lambda}} \in \{0, 0.01, \ldots, max\{\hat{\lambda}_i\}\}$

Table 2 shows the respective parameter values. Please note that finding the best parameter settings for QSD and QLD has to be taken with some caution. With this optimization we can only show that these methods have the potential to obtain a specific performance.

Table 2. Optimal Parameter Settings

		CACM	CISI	CRAN	CR-title	CR-desc	CR-narr	FR	AP90*
PRF	α	1.7	0.7	1.3	0.6	0.5	0.4	0.6	0.2
	θ	0.35	0.7	0.9	0.75	0.85	0.95	0.55	0.75
QSD	ϑ	0.24	0.41	0.49	0.42	0.44	0.33	0.36	0.68
QLD	ϑ	0.22	0.25	0.37	0.41	0.36	0.17	0.37	0.68
	$\vartheta_{\hat{\lambda}}$	0.16	0.23	0.41	0.43	0.37	0.20	0.13	0.48
TCL	-	-	-	-	-	-	-	-	-
PRF(QSD)	ϑ	same as for QSD							
	α	0.6	0.3	0.7	0.6	0.5	0.4	0.4	0.1
	θ	0.65	0.7	0.95	0.75	0.85	0.95	0.0	0.9
PRF(QLD)	$\vartheta, \vartheta_{\hat{\lambda}}$	same as for QLD							
	α	0.8	0.2	0.6	0.4	0.5	0.4	0.4	0.1
	θ	0.7	0.85	0.95	0.75	0.85	0.95	0.0	0.9
PRF(TCL)	α	1.9	0.2	0.4	0.6	0.3	0.0	0.3	0.1
	θ	0.70	0.85	0.90	0.85	0.95	0.00	0.45	0.95

Table 3 shows the average precision obtained by using the best parameter values for different methods. The best value of the average precision is indicated in bold face. Figures 2 to 4 show the corresponding recall/precision graphs. The results of the significance tests are shown in table 4. The entries have the following meanings with respect to the two methods X and Y:

- $\gg$ (>) indicates that X performs better than Y at the significance level of $\alpha = 0.01$ ($\alpha = 0.05$)
- $\ll$ (<) indicates that X performs worse than Y at the significance level of $\alpha = 0.01$ ($\alpha = 0.05$).
- $\circ$ indicates that no statement on differences can be made on the significance levels.

Our findings are as follows:

- The results show that with the optimal parameter setting PRF always performs better than the pure VSM model in our test sets.
- The QSD and QLD approaches generally also outperform the VSM with just one exception being not significant (QSD on "CR-desc"). The comparison between TCL and VSM gives no clear picture.

Table 3. Average precision obtained in different methods

	CACM	CISI	CRAN	CR-title	CR-desc	CR-narr	FR	AP90*
VSM	13.0	12.0	38.4	13.5	17.5	17.3	8.5	74.3
PRF	19.9	12.9	43.5	16.9	20.4	19.2	11.3	75.5
QSD	23.7	14.2	42.8	15.2	17.2	17.3	10.9	81.1
QLD	22.7	17.1	43.6	16.4	17.5	17.5	10.8	81.1
TCL	28.2	10.0	34.2	16.0	16.7	8.2	14.0	62.9
PRF(QSD)	25.7	14.5	45.1	19.5	19.1	17.7	16.3	**81.4**
PRF(QLD)	27.3	**17.3**	**45.3**	**20.4**	19.2	**18.4**	16.1	**81.4**
PRF(TCL)	**30.4**	12.7	42.6	18.0	**20.6**	17.3	**19.9**	77.3

Table 4. Comparison of approaches using significance test

X	Y	CACM	CISI	CRAN	CR-title	CR-desc	CR-narr	FR	AP90*
PRF	VSM	≫	≫	≫	>	≫	>	>	>
QSD	VSM	≫	>	≫	o	o	o	>	≫
QLD	VSM	≫	≫	≫	o	o	o	>	≫
TCL	VSM	≫	≪	≪	≫	o	≪	≫	≪
QSD	PRF	o	o	o	o	≪	<	o	≫
QLD	PRF	o	≫	o	o	≪	o	o	≫
TCL	PRF	≫	≪	≪	o	o	≪	o	≪
PRF(QSD)	PRF	o	o	o	o	<	o	>	≫
PRF(QLD)	PRF	>	≫	o	o	o	o	>	≫
PRF(TCL)	PRF	≫	o	o	o	o	<	≫	>

- The combined methods generally outperform VSM and PRF as expected. Two exceptions are PRF(QSD) as compared to PRF on "CR-desc" and PRF(TCL) as compared to PRF on "CR-narr". In these two settings the combined methods are significantly worse than PRF.
- As expected QLD slightly outperforms QSD in most cases. This is also true for the combined version PRF(QLD) which mostly outperforms PRF(QSD).
- Generally, the best results are obtained with the approaches combining QLD, QSD, and TCL with PRF.

We did some analysis in order to explain the different performances of our approaches in the collections taking the properties of the test set into account. So far, we have not been able to find a clear correlation between measurable properties of the test sets and the results. We expect the following factors to be crucial for good results:

- the query lengths
- the overlap of "query content" in a test collection (number of queries and extent of overlap)
- the number of relevant documents for queries with some "overlap in content"

8 Summary

We expect that a real world information retrieval system has a relatively large overlap in user interests and queries. In Collaborative Information Retrieval (CIR) we want to benefit from this overlap by exploiting users search processes for subsequent searches. As an initial step towards techniques we focused on a restricted CIR scenario in which only user queries and the relevant answer documents to these queries are known. The three approaches QSD, QLD, and TCL that we developed for this scenario were tested on queries of standard Information Retrieval test collections. Although in these collections we do not have the query and interest distribution that we assume to have in real world systems, the approaches show relatively good results, in particular if they are combined with pseudo relevance feedback. It turns out that the QLD, an extension of the QSD approach, performs slightly better. The differences between QLD and TCL give no clear picture. We are still lacking on an explanation when and why TCL or QLD performs better or worse.

As one of our next steps for the QSD/QLD approaches we want to learn the similarity measure between queries based on training examples. In future, for the TCL approach, we do not always want to extend query terms by learned concepts but only if the learned concepts are reliable in some way. Two more topics that we will work on in the future are the removal of the explicit parameters in the QSD and QLD approach as well as shifting towards real world retrieval systems. For the latter we are cooperating with a search engine provider.

Acknowledgements

This work was supported by the German Ministry for Education and Research, BMBF (Grant: 01 IN 902 B8).

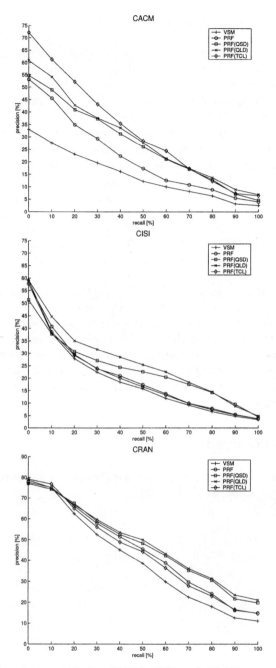

Fig. 2. Recall/precision graphs for CACM, CISI, and CRAN.

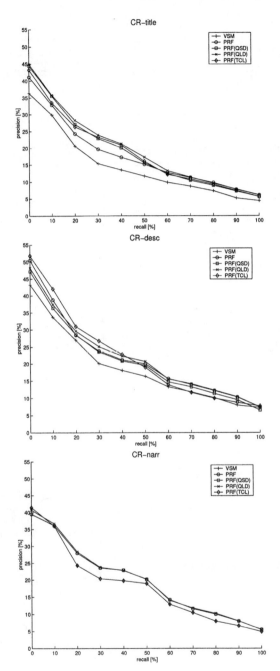

Fig. 3. Recall/precision graphs for CR.

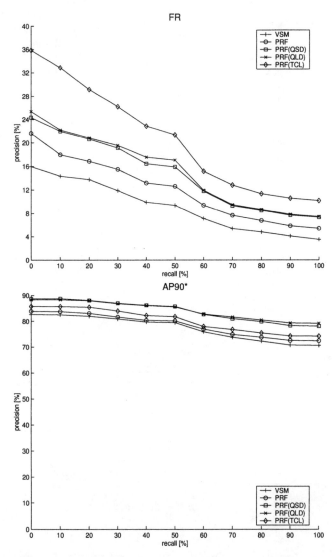

Fig. 4. Recall/precision graphs for FR and AP90*.

References

1. R. Baeza-Yates and B. Ribeiro-Neto. *Modern Information Retrieval.* Addison-Wesley Publishing Company, 1999.
2. C. Buckley, G. Salton, and J. Allen. The effect of adding relevance information in a relevance feedback environment. In *Proceedings of the 17th Annual International ACM-SIGIR Conference on Research and Development in Information Retrieval,* pages 292–300, Dublin, Ireland, 1994.
3. H. Cui, J. Wen, J. Nie, and W. Ma. Probabilistic Query Expansion Using Query Logs. In *Proceedings of the Eleventh International World Wide Web Conference (WWW2002),* Honolulu, Hawaii, USA, 2002.
4. D. Hull. Using statistical testing in the evaluation of retrieval experiments. In *Proceedings of the 16th Annual International ACM-SIGIR Conference on Research and Development in Information Retrieval,* pages 329–338, Pittsburgh, PA, USA, 1993.
5. K. Kise, M. Junker, A. Dengel, and K. Matsumoto. Experimental Evaluation of Passage-Based Document Retrieval. In *Proceedings of the Sixth International Conference on Document Analysis and Recognition (ICDAR'01),* pages 592–596, Seattle, Washington, USA, 2001.
6. C. Manning and H. Schütze. *Foundations of Natural Language Processing.* MIT Press, 1999.
7. Y. Qiu and H.-P. Frei. Concept-based query expansion. In *Proceedings of the 16th Annual International ACM-SIGIR Conference on Research and Development in Information Retrieval,* pages 160–169, Pittsburgh, PA, USA, 1993.
8. ftp://ftp.cs.cornell.edu/pub/smart.
9. J.J. Rocchio. Relevance feedback in information retrieval. In *The SMART Retrieval System - Experiments in Automatic Document Processing,* pages 313–323. Prentice Hall, Englewood Cliffs, N.J., 1971.
10. http://trec.nist.gov.
11. E. M. Voorhees and D. Harman. Overview of the ninth text retrieval conference (TREC-9). In *Proceedings of the Ninth Text Retrieval Conference,* pages 1–13, Gaithersburg, Maryland, USA, 2000.
12. Y. Yang and X. Liu. A re-examination of text categorization methods. In *Proceedings of the 22nd Annual International ACM-SIGIR Conference on Research and Development in Information Retrieval,* pages 42–49, University of California, Berkeley, USA, 1999.

The XDOC Document Suite - a Workbench for Document Mining

Dietmar Rösner and Manuela Kunze

Otto-von-Guericke-Universität Magdeburg
Institut für Wissens- und Sprachverarbeitung
P.O.box 4120, 39016 Magdeburg, Germany
{roesner, makunze}@iws.cs.uni-magdeburg.de

Abstract. We report about the current state of development of the XDOC document suite and its applications. This collection of tools for the flexible and robust processing of documents in German is based on the use of XML as unifying formalism. XML is used not only for encoding input and output data but as well for capturing process information and for the flexible encoding of resources (lexica, grammar rules, semantic mappings etc.). XDOC is organized in modules with limited responsibilities that can easily be combined into pipelines to solve complex tasks. Strong emphasis is laid on a number of techniques to deal with lexical and conceptual gaps that are typical when starting a new application.

1 Introduction

Collections of documents can be a valuable source of knowledge. It is worthwhile to invest in efforts to get access to these sources. On the other hand human document processing alone will not suffice and is both costly and slow. Therefore any support offered by automatic analysis tools and techniques like document mining will be highly appreciated. This is the general motivation for the work reported in this paper: the design and implementation of the XDOC document suite as a workbench for the flexible processing of electronically available documents in German.

The XDOC document workbench is currently employed in a number of applications. These include:

- knowledge acquisition from technical documentation about casting technology,
- extraction of company profiles from WWW pages,
- analysis of autopsy protocols.

Our work is driven by such applications but of course we try to work out solutions that are abstract and general enough and have a high potential to be transferable to other tasks in document processing as well as other domains. [1]

---

[1] We even experiment with transfer to other languages: [Kunze and Xiao, 2002] reports about an experiment with English resources for XDOC for the task of text mining from English documents.

In the following we will work out the architecture of the XDOC toolbox for document analysis based on natural language processing (nlp). We will concentrate on the subtasks to be solved and the problems to be tackled. This will be accompanied in many cases by a sketch of the solution chosen in our system. The solution will be explained with examples of data and analysis results from a variety of domains. Whenever appropriate we will highlight shortcomings and open problems or discuss the pros and cons of alternative design decisions. Emphasis will be laid on elaborating both on the algorithms employed as well as on the resources that have to be provided.

2   Design Principles for XDOC

XDOC stands for *X*ML based tools for *doc*ument processing. We have decided to exploit XML [Bray et al., 1998] and its accompanying formalisms (e.g. XSLT [Site, 2002b]) and tools (e.g. xt [Clark, 2002]) as a unifying framework. All modules in the XDOC system expect XML documents as input and deliver their results in XML format.

We are interested in tools and techniques for natural language analysis that help humans with their document processing tasks. The end users of our applications are domain experts (e.g. medical doctors, engineers, ...). They are interested in getting their problems solved but they are typically neither interested nor trained in computational linguistics. Therefore the barrier they will have to overcome before they can use a computational linguistic or text technology system should be as low as possible. This constraint has consequences for the design of the document suite.

XML is an excellent basis to realize the design goals for XDOC. These include:

- The tools shall not only be usable by developers but as well by domain experts without linguistic training.
  Here again XML and XSLT play a major role: XSL stylesheets can be exploited to allow different presentations of internal data and results for different target groups; for end users the internals are in many cases not helpful, whereas developers will need them for debugging.
- The tools should be usable independently but should allow for flexible combination and interoperability.
  Document mining is an experimental activity. This is especially true when you start processing documents in a new corpus and in a formerly unknown domain. This is the scenario in which users should profit most from XDOC.
- The tools should be as robust as possible.
  In general it can not be expected that lexicon information is available for all tokens in a document. This is not only the case for most tokens from 'nonlexical' types – like telephone numbers, enzyme names, material codes, ... –, even for lexical types there will always be 'lexical gaps'. This

may either be caused by neologisms or simply by starting to process documents from a new application domain with a new sublanguage. In the latter case lexical items will typically be missing in the lexicon ('lexical gap') and phrasal structures may not or not adequately be covered by the grammar ('syntax gap'). In addition the domain model will typically need elaboration ('conceptual gap').

- The tools should be usable for all sorts of 'realistic' documents.
  One aspect of 'realistic' documents is that they typically contain domain specific tokens which are not directly covered by classical lexical categories (like noun, verb, ...). Those tokens are nevertheless often essential for the user of the document (e.g. an enzyme descriptor like EC 4.1.1.17 for a biochemist).

2.1   Some Remarks about XML and NLP

XML – and its precursor SGML – offers a formalism to annotate pieces of (natural language) texts. To be more precise: If a text is (as a simple first approximation) seen as a sequence of characters (alphabetic and whitespace characters) then XML allows to associate arbitrary markup with arbitrary subsequences of *contiguous* characters. Many units of interest for natural language analysis (nlp) are represented by strings of contiguous characters (e.g. words, phrases, clauses etc.). It is a straightforward idea to use XML to encode information about such a substring of a text interpreted as a meaningful linguistic unit and to associate this information directly with the occurrence of the unit in the text. The basic idea of annotation is further backed by XML's wellformedness demand that XML elements have to be properly nested. This is fully concordant with standard linguistic practice: complex structures are made up from simpler structures covering substrings of the full string in a nested way.

3   A Reference Model

Document mining is just one possible application of document processing. An incomplete list of other applications of document analysis includes among others information retrieval (IR), information extraction (IE), web mining, text classification , summarization, machine translation, concept learning, etc. Each of these applications has its specific demands. Nevertheless they share many of their subtasks. For a given complex application in document processing we found it fruitful to distinguish its subtaks into two categories:

- subtasks that are relevant for all nlp approaches to document processing,
- subtasks that are specific for the application.

This paper has its focus on the first group of subtasks. Since these subtasks are shared as well with other applications of document processing there is a high potential for reuse and resource sharing for these subtasks. At best complex applications should be configurable from a common tool box with generic modules and generic resources in combination with only a small number of dedicated application specific modules.

For the information extraction task Hobbs (1995) has specified a 'Generic IE System' as a set of modules and he has argued that most implemented IE systems will draw their modules from this set.

We give a short sketch of the functionality captured in these modules (cf. pp 252 in [Cowie and Wilks, 2000]):[2]

- text zoning: select those parts from the document that will be subjected to further processing
- preprocessing: determine sentence boundaries in the text and within sentences determine word boundaries
- filtering: in the set of sentences filter those that are irrelevant
- preparsing: recognize proper names, numbers, dates and other regularly formed constructions
- parsing: takes a set of lexical items (single words or multi-word phrases) and outputs a syntactic analysis in the form of parse tree fragments
- fragment combination: attempt to combine fragments to cover whole sentences
- semantic interpretation: generate semantic structures from parse tree fragments
- lexical disambiguation: what is the correct lexical sense of a lexical item with multiple senses?
- coreference resolution: identify different descriptions of the same entity as corefential
- template generation: the result structure for IE, also called template, has to be filled with semantic structures

It should be emphasized that this is a functional distinction and primarily serves as a reference model. Implemented systems do not necessarily realize each function in a distinct module. Moreover the order of the presentation should not be misinterpreted as a fixed order for the realization of the functions. Lexical disambiguation may e.g. occur within a number of possible places in the overall process. In addition the functions differ strongly with respect to both domain- and task-independence. For example template generation is an IE specific module; the modules dealing with semantic issues – i.e. semantic interpretation, lexical disambiguation, coreference resolution – are far more domain dependent than those dealing with preprocessing and syntax.

---

[2] The relation (and differences) between these generic modules and the implemented functionality in XDOC (as discussed below) should be obvious.

4   A Closer Look at XDOC

We will discuss the tools in the XDOC document suite according to the following functional grouping:

- preprocessing,
- structure detection,
- POS tagging,
- syntactic parsing,
- semantic analysis.

For each application these generic tools have to be complemented with tools for the specific application.

4.1   Preprocessing

Tools for preprocessing are used to convert documents from a number of formats (e.g. DVI, Postscript, pdf, doc, rtf, etc.) into the XML format amenable for further processing. As a subtask this includes treatment of special characters (e.g. for umlauts, apostrophes, ...).

For linguistic processing we are primarily interested in the sequence of characters constituting the paper's natural language content (i.e. the plain text). The process of mapping from an arbitrary format of the document source to the input representation for linguistic processing may be conceptualized either as 'stripping off' non-text (i.e. commands, mark up, ...) or as extracting text. In either case this process has to preserve that information from the source that is relevant for further processing.

This information to preserve or 'carry over' deals with issues like:

- What is a unit of linguistic relevance?
- Where are boundaries between units?
- What is the function of those boundaries?

The result of this preprocessing step should preserve and make explicit (e.g. mark up) this structural information in addition to the linguistic content (i.e. the character sequence of the plain text). This requirement holds independent of the specific format of the source.

4.2   Structure Detection

We accept raw ASCII texts without any markup as input as well. Raw ASCII may be the original source, it is as well the output of many publicly available converters like l2a, pdf2text, etc. In such cases structure detection tries to uncover linguistic units (e.g. sentences, titles, etc.) as candidates for further analysis. A major subtask is to identify the role of punctuation characters.

If we have the structures in a text explicitly available this may be exploited by subsequent linguistic processing. An example: For a unit classified as title or subtitle you will accept a noun phrase ('The catcher in the rye') or a prepositional phrase ('In defense of logic') whereas within a paragraph you will expect full sentences.

In realistic texts even the detection of possible sentence boundaries needs some care. A period character may not only be used as a full stop but may as well be part of an abbreviation (e.g. 'z.B.' – engl.: 'e.g.' – or 'Dr.'), be contained in a number (3.14), be used in an email address or in domain specific tokens. Example 1 serves to illustrate this point (IP is used for punctuation and ABBR for abbreviations).

Example 1. Structure detection and POS tagging: abbreviations and unknown words

```
XDOC(4): (tag-text "Begruessung: Prof. Dr. Gholamreza Nakhaeizadeh")

"<N SRC="UNG">Begruessung</N><IP>:</IP> <ABBR>Prof.</ABBR> <ABBR>Dr.</ABBR>
<N SRC="UC1">Gholamreza</N> <N SRC="UC1">Nakhaeizadeh</N>
"
```

4.3   POS Tagging

The assignment of part-of-speech information to a token - POS tagging for short - is not only a preparatory step for parsing. The information gained about a document by POS tagging and evaluating its results is valuable in its own right. The ratio of tokens not classifiable by the POS tagger to tokens classified is a direct indication of the degree of lexical coverage.

In principle a number of approaches is usable for POS tagging (e.g. [Brill, 1992]). We decided to avoid approaches based on (supervised) learning from tagged corpora, since the cost for creating the necessary training data are likely to be prohibitive for our users (especially in specialized sublanguages).

The approach chosen was to try to make best use of available resources for German and to enhance them with additional functionalities. The tool chosen (MORPHIX [Finkler and Neumann, 1988]) is not only used in POS tagging but serves as a general morphosyntactic component for German.

The resources employed in XDOC's POS tagger are:

- the lexicon and the inflectional analysis from the morphosyntactic component MORPHIX
- a number of heuristics (e.g. for the classification of token not covered in the lexicon)

For German the morphology component MORPHIX has been developed in a number of projects and is available in different realisations. This component has the advantage that the *closed* class lexical items of German - e.g. determiners, prepositions, pronouns, etc. - as well as all irregular verbs are fully covered. The coverage of *open* class lexical items is dependent on the amount of lexical coding. The paradigms for e.g. verb conjugation and noun declination are fully covered. To be able to analyze and generate word forms, however, their roots and their classification need to be included in the MORPHIX lexicon.

We exploit MORPHIX - in addition to its role in syntactic parsing - for POS tagging as well. If a token in a German text can be morphologically analyzed with MORPHIX, the resulting word class categorisation is used as POS information. Note that this classification need not be unique. Since the tokens are analyzed in isolation, multiple analyses are often the case. Some examples: the token *'das'* may either be a determiner (with a number of different combinations for the features case, number and gender) or a relative pronoun, the token *'schoene'* may be either an adjective or – less likely, but possible – a verb (again with different feature combinations not relevant for POS tagging).

Since we do not expect extensive lexicon coding at the beginning of an XDOC application some tokens will not get a MORPHIX analysis. We then employ two techniques: We first try to make use of heuristics that are based on aspects of the tokens that can easily be detected with simple string analysis (e.g. upper-/lowercase, endings, etc.) and/or exploitation of the token position relative to sentence boundaries (detected in the structure detection module). If a heuristic yields a classification the resulting POS class is added together with the name of the employed heuristic (marked as feature SRC, cf. example 1). If no heuristics are applicable we classify the token as member of the class unknown (tagged with **XXX**).

To keep the POS tagger fast and simple, the disambiguation between multiple POS classes for a token and the derivation of a possible POS class from context for an unknown token are postponed until syntactic processing. This is in line with our general principle to accept results with overgeneration when a module is applied in isolation (here: POS tagging) and to rely on filtering ambiguous results in a later stage of processing (here: exploiting the syntactic context).

Example 2. Domain-specific tagging

```
<PRODUCT Method="Sandguss" Material="CC333G">
    <N>Gussstueck</N>
    <NORM>
        <N>EN</N>
        <NR>1982</NR>
    </NORM>
    <IP>-</IP>
    <MAT-ID>CC333G</MAT-ID>
    <IP>-</IP>
    <METHODE>GS</METHODE>
    <IP>-</IP>
    <MODELLNR>XXXX</MODELLNR>
</PRODUCT>
```

The example above is the result of tagging domain-specific identifier. The token is annotated as a *PRODUCT* element with a description of the used method and material as attributes. It is a typical token in the metal casting domain.

4.4   Syntactic Parsing

For syntactic parsing we apply a chart parser based on context free grammar rules augmented with feature structures. The resulting parse trees are encoded in a straightforward XML format (cf. example 3). Morphosyntactic features (e.g. gender, number and case as GEN, NUM and CAS resp.) as well as processing information (e.g. the name of the rule employed in attribute RULE) are encoded in attribute values.

Example 3. Excerpt from a syntactic analysis

```
<PP CAS="AKK">
  <PRP CAS="AKK">durch</PRP>
  <NP TYPE="COMPLEX" RULE="NPC1" GEN="NTR" NUM="SG" CAS="AKK">
    <NP TYPE="FULL" RULE="NP1" CAS="AKK" NUM="SG" GEN="NTR">
      <N>Schaffen</N>
    </NP>
    <NP TYPE="FULL" RULE="NP2" CAS="GEN" NUM="SG" GEN="MAS">
      <DETD>des</DETD>
      <N>Zusammenhalts</N>
    </NP>
  </NP>
</PP>
```

Again robustness is achieved by allowing as input elements:

- multiple POS classes,
- unknown tokens of open world classes and
- tokens with POS class, but without or only partial feature information.

Example 4. Unknown token classified as noun with heuristics

```
<NP TYPE="COMPLEX" RULE="NPC3" GEN="FEM"
        NUM="PL" CAS="_">
  <NP TYPE="FULL" RULE="NP1" CAS="_" NUM="PL" GEN="FEM">
    <N SRC="UNG">Blutanhaftungen</N>
  </NP>
  <PP CAS="DAT">
    <PRP CAS="DAT">an</PRP>
    <NP TYPE="FULL" RULE="NP2" CAS="DAT" NUM="SG" GEN="FEM">
      <DETD>der</DETD>
      <N SRC="UC1">Gekroesewurzel</N>
    </NP>
  </PP>
</NP>
```

The latter case results from some heuristics in POS tagging that allow to assume e.g. the class noun for a token but do not suffice to detect its full paradigm from the token (note that there are ca two dozen different morphosyntactic paradigms for noun declination in German).

For a given input the parser attempts to find all complete analyses that cover the input. If no such complete analysis is achievable it tries to combine maximal partial results ('chunks') into structures covering the whole input.

A successful analysis may be based on an assumption about the word class of an initially unclassified token (tagged XXX). This is indicated in the parsing result (feature AS) and can be exploited for learning such classifications from contextual constraints. In a similar way the successful combination

of known feature values from closed class items (e.g. determiners, prepositions) with underspecified features (written as '_' in attribute-value-pairs)
in agreement constraints allows the determination of paradigm information
from successfully processed occurrences. See example 5: In the input string
the word *'Mundhoehle'* (oral cavity) was not available in the lexicon. Because
it is uppercase and not at sentence initial position it is heuristically classified
as noun. The successful parse of the prepositional phrase *'in der Mundhoehle'*
allows to derive features from the determiner within the PP (e.g. the lexical
gender feminine for *'Mundhoehle'*).

Example 5. An unknown token classified as adjective and features derived
through contextual constraints:

```
<NP TYPE="COMPLEX" RULE="NPC3" GEN="MAS" NUM="SG" CAS="NOM">
  <NP TYPE="FULL" RULE="NP3" CAS="NOM" NUM="SG" GEN="MAS">
    <DETI>kein</DETI>
    <XXX AS="ADJ">ungehoeriger</XXX>
    <N>Inhalt</N>
  </NP>
  <PP CAS="DAT">
    <PRP CAS="DAT">in</PRP>
    <NP TYPE="FULL" RULE="NP2" CAS="DAT" NUM="SG" GEN="FEM">
      <DETD>der</DETD>
      <N SRC="UC1">Mundhoehle</N>
    </NP>
  </PP>
</NP>"
```

The grammar used in syntactic parsing is organised in a modular way that
allows to add or remove groups of rules. This is exploited when the sublanguage of a domain contains linguistic structures that are unusual or even
ungrammatical in standard German.

4.5   Semantic Analysis

At the time of writing semantic analysis uses three methods:

Semantic Tagging. For semantic tagging we apply a semantic lexicon.
This lexicon contains the semantic interpretation of a token and a case frame
combined with the syntactic valence requirements. Similar to POS tagging
the tokens are annotated with their meaning and a classification in semantic categories like e.g. concepts and relations. Again it is possible, that the
classification of a token in isolation is not unique. Multiple classification can
be resolved through the following analysis of the case frame and through its
combination with the syntactic structure which includes the token.

Analysis of Case Frames. By the case frame analysis of a token we obtain
details about the type of recognized concepts (resolving multiple interpreta-
tions) and possible relations to other concepts. The results are tagged with
XML tags. We use attributes to show the description of the concepts and

we can annotate the relevant relations between the concepts through nested tags.

Example 6. Excerpt from a case frame analysis

```
<CONCEPT TYPE=Prozess>
    <WORD>Fertigen</WORD>
    <DESC>Schaffung von etwas</DESC>
    <SLOT>
        <RESULT FORM="N(gen, fak) P(akk, fak, von)">fester Koerper</result>
        <SOURCE FORM="P(dat, fak, aus)">aus formlosem Stoff </source>
        <INSTRUMENT FORM="P(akk, fak, durch)">durch Schaffen des Zusammenhalts</instrument>
    </SLOT>
</CONCEPT>
```

The example above is part of the result of the analysis of the German phrase: *Fertigen fester Koerper aus formlosem Stoff durch Schaffen des Zusammenhalts*[3]. The token *Fertigen* is classified as *process* with the relations *source*, *result* and *instrument*. The following phrases (noun phrases and preposition phrases) are checked to make sure they are assignable to the relation requirements (semantic and syntactic) of the token *Fertigen*.

Semantic Interpretation of the Syntactic Structure. Another step to analyze the relations between tokens can be the interpretation of the syntactic structure of a phrase or sentence respectively. We exploit the syntactic structure of the sublanguage to extract the relation between co-occurring tokens. For example a typical phrase from an autopsy report: *Leber dunkelrot.*[4]

Semantic tagging results in the following structure:

Example 7. Result of semantic tagging

```
<CONCEPT TYPE="organ">Leber</CONCEPT>
<PROPERTY TYPE="color">dunkelrot</PROPERTY>
<XXX>.</XXX>
```

In this example we can extract the relation "has-color" between the tokens *Leber* and *dunkelrot*.

4.6   Current State and Future Work

The XDOC document workbench is currently employed in a number of applications. These include:

- knowledge acquisition from technical documentation about casting technology,
- extraction of company profiles from WWW pages,
- analysis of autopsy protocols.

---

[3] In English: production of solid objects from formless matter by creating cohesion
[4] In English: Liver dark red.

The latter application is part of a joint project with the institute for forensic medicine of our university. The medical doctors there are interested in tools that help them to exploit their huge collection of several thousand autopsy protocols for their research interests. The confrontation with this corpus has stimulated experiments with what we now call 'bootstrapping techniques' for lexicon and ontology creation ([Rösner and Kunze, 2002]).

The core idea of 'bootstrapping' is the following:

When you are confronted with a new corpus from a new domain, try to find linguistic structures in the text that are easy to detect automatically and that allow to classify unknown terms in a robust manner both syntactically as well as on the knowledge level. Take the results from a run of these simple but robust heuristics as an initial version of a domain dependent lexicon and ontology. Exploit these initial resources to extend the processing to more complicated linguistic structures in order to detect and classify more terms of interest automatically.

An example: In the sublanguage of autopsy protocols (in German) a very telegrammatic style is dominant. Condensed and compact structures like the following are very frequent:

Example 8. Autopsy protocols: telegrammatic style

```
Harnblase leer.
Harnleiter frei.
Nierenoberflaeche glatt.
Vorsteherdruese altersentsprechend.
...
```

These structures can be abstracted syntactically as the simple pattern

<Noun><Adjective><Fullstop>

and semantically as

<Anatomic-entity><Attribute-value>.

In addition they are easily detectable.

In our experiments we have exploited this characteristic of the corpus extensively to automatically deduce an initial lexicon (with nouns and adjectives) and ontology (with concepts for anatomic regions or organs and their respective features and values). The feature values were further exploited to cluster the concept candidates into groups according to their feature values. In this way container like entities with feature values like 'leer' (empty) or 'gefuellt' (full) can be distinguished from e.g. entities of surface type with feature values like 'glatt' (smooth).

5   Related Work

The work in XDOC has been inspired by a number of precursory projects:

124   Rösner, Kunze

In GATE [Site, 2002a,Cunningham and Wilks, 1988] the idea of piping simple modules in order to achieve complex functionality has been applied to NLP with such a rigid architecture for the first time. The project LT XML has been pioneering XML as a data format for linguistic processing.

Both GATE and LT XML [Group, 1999] were employed for processing English texts. SMES [Neumann et al., 1997] has been an attempt to develop a toolbox for message extraction from German texts. A disadvantage of SMES that is avoided in XDOC is the lack of a uniform encoding formalism, in other words, users are confronted with different formats in each module.

System Availability

Major components of XDOC are made publicly accessible for testing and experiments under the URL:
http://lima.cs.uni-magdeburg.de:8000/

Summary

We have reported about the current state of the XDOC document suite. This collection of tools for the flexible and robust processing of documents in German is based on the use of XML as unifying formalism for encoding input and output data as well as process information. It is organized in modules with limited responsibilities that can easily be combined into pipelines to solve complex tasks. Strong emphasis is laid on a number of techniques to deal with lexical and conceptual gaps.

References

[Bray et al., 1998] T. Bray, J. Paoli, and C.M. Sperberg-McQueen (1998) Extensible Markup Language (XML) 1.0. *http://www.w3.org/TR/1998/REC-xml-19980210*

[Brill, 1992] E. Brill (1992) A simple rule-based part-of-speech tagger. In *Proceeding of the Third Conference on Applied Natural Language Processing*, pages 152–155

[Clark, 2002] J. Clark (2002) http://www.jclark.com

[Cowie and Wilks, 2000] J. Cowie and Y. Wilks (2000) Information Extraction. In R. Dale, H. Moisl, and H. Somers, editors, *Handbook of Natual Language Processing*, pages 241–260, New York. Marcel Dekker Inc

[Cunningham and Wilks, 1988] H. Cunningham and Y. Wilks (1988) GATE - a General Architecture for Text Engineering. *Proccedings of COLING-96*. http://gate.ac.uk

[Finkler and Neumann, 1988] W. Finkler and G. Neumann (1988) MORPHIX: a fast Realization of a classification-based Approach to Morphology. In H. Trost, editor, *Proc. der 4. Österreichischen Artificial-Intelligence Tagung, Wiener Workshop Wissensbasierte Sprachverarbeitung*, pages 11–19. Springer Verlag

[Group, 1999] Language Technology Group   (1999)   LT XML version 1.1.
http://www.ltg.ed.ac.uk/software/xml/

[Kunze and Xiao, 2002] M. Kunze and C. Xiao (2002) An Approach for Resource Sharing in Multilingual NLP.(Poster). In T. Vidal and P. Liberatore, editors, *Proceedings of STarting Artificial Intelligence Researchers Symposium STAIRS 2002*, volume 78 of *Frontiers in Artificial Intelligence and Applications*, IOS Press Amsterdam

[Neumann et al., 1997] G. Neumann, R. Backofen, J. Baur, M. Becker, and C. Braun (1997) An information extraction core system for real world german text processing. pages 208–215

[Rösner and Kunze, 2002] D. Rösner and M. Kunze (2002) Exploiting sublanguage and domain characteristics in a bootstrapping approach to lexicon and ontology creation. In *Proceedings of the OntoLex 2002 - Ontologies and Lexical Knowledge Bases at the LREC 2002*, pages 68–73, Las Palmas

[Site, 2002a] GATE Site (2002) http://gate.ac.uk

[Site, 2002b] XSL Site (2002) http://www.w3.org/style/xsl

Appendix: Interaction with XDOC

The following short series of screenshots is intended to give an impression of the interaction with the web based interface of XDOC.

For a better readability of the screenshots we have chosen here a simple presentation of the results. In practice the results are highlighted with different colors.

Input to XDOC can either be typed in directly (appropriate for short tests) or loaded from the file system. In addition a number of example sentences illustrating the range of linguistic structures covered are available as a tutorial for unexperienced users.

For the current text functions like structure detection, POS tagging, syntactic parsing, semantic annotation can be started from the menu on the left and the processing results are displayed in the central output area. In many cases a variety of display formats is offered.

For illustration purposes we use the simple example sentence: 'Die Regierungsmitglieder beglueckwuenschten die Frauen.' Here the words 'Regierungsmitglieder' and 'beglueckwuenschten' are unknown. As an uppercase word the first is classified during POS tagging as a noun (cf. figure 1). The parser finds four possible readings, all under the assumption that 'beglueckwuenschten' is a finite verb. The parsing result in full detail is given in figure 2, a more compact presentation of the same result shows figure 3.

Of course full texts can be processed as well. As an example we use the web page of a metal casting company. Here the results of POS tagging are given in figure 4 and those of a domain specific classification of terms in figure 5.

Fig. 1. Results of the POS tagger.

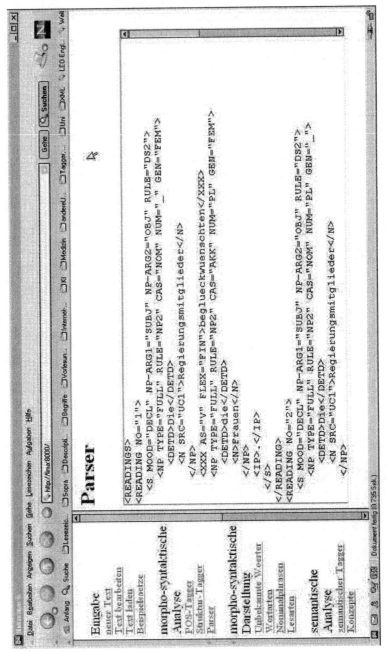

Fig. 2. Complete results of the chart parser

128   Rösner, Kunze

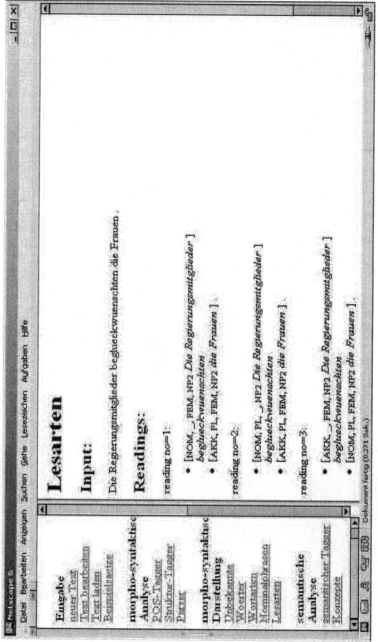

Fig. 3. Presentation of readings

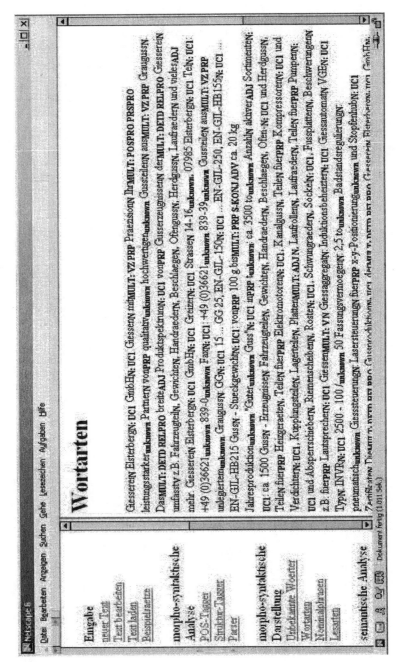

Fig. 4. Wordclasses inside a casting domain text.

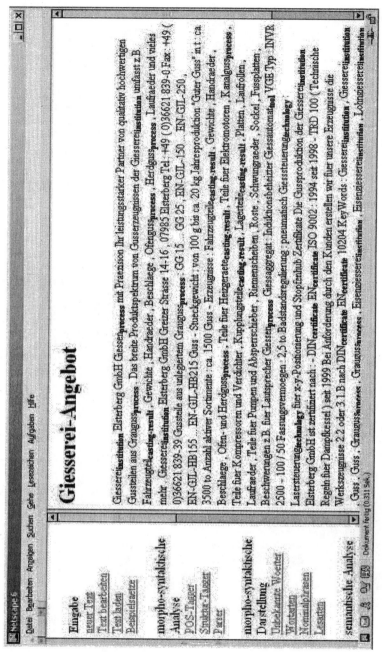

Fig. 5. Annotated domain specific terms

On Knowledgeable Unsupervised Text Mining

Andreas Hotho[1], Alexander Maedche[2], Steffen Staab[1,3],
and Valentin Zacharias[2]

[1] Forschungszentrum Informatik at the Univ. Karlsruhe,
D-76131 Karlsruhe, Germany
{maedche, zach}@fzi.de,

http://www.fzi.de/WIM

[2] Institute AIFB, Univ. Karlsruhe,
D-76128 Karlsruhe, Germany
{hotho, staab}@aifb.uni-karlsruhe.de,

http://www.aifb.uni-karlsruhe.de/WBS

[3] Ontoprise GmbH
D-76131 Karlsruhe, Germany
staab@ontoprise.de,

http://www.ontoprise.de

Abstract. Text Mining is about discovering novel, interesting and useful patterns from textual data. In this paper we discuss several means that introduce background knowledge into unsupervised text mining in order to improve the novelty, the interestingness or the usefulness of the detected patterns. Germane to the different proposals is that they strive for higher abstractions that carry more explanatory power and more possibilities for exploring the input texts than is achievable by unknowledgeable means.

1 Introduction

Knowledge discovery is concerned with finding novel, interesting and useful patterns in data. In order to successfully discover such patterns, it is necessary that the data that is investigated is structured in a way accessible to machine learning algorithms. Texts, however, do not show much structure to the eye of the naive machine learning algorithm. Only in the eye of the human beholder, text documents exhibit the rich linguistic and conceptual structures that may let him discover patterns that are not explicit.[1] Based on these considerations we may conjecture that in order to improve the effectiveness and utility of machine learning on texts, we must improve the linguistic and/or the conceptual background knowledge available to machine

---

[1] In fact, in the eye of the linguist, texts show a much richer structure than databases because texts are mostly self-explanatory, while databases typically aren't.

learning algorithms and we must actively exploit it. We argue that unsupervised machine learning algorithms are greatly handicapped when trying to detect patterns. In contrast to supervised machine learning methods, they cannot even fall back to guidance coming from the training examples when exploring the vast extents of words.

Therefore, we have investigated new methods that apply unsupervised machine learning algorithms and take advantage of linguistic and conceptual background knowledge. In this paper, we focus on the description and application of conceptual background knowledge given by ontologies.

The gist of our approaches can be described as combining shallow information extracting methods in order to map (some) words to their conceptual descriptions, to use the ontology for abstracting text representations to various higher levels of granularity and then to apply conventional machine learning techniques. Finally, the ontologies are also used for communicating and presenting the results to the users.

Organization. The organization of the paper is as follows. First, we provide an introduction to our overall conceptual architecture. We introduce the main components and their relationships. Furthermore, we give a short description of the formal structures we use for defining the ontologies and instances and their interrelationships with the lexicon. Section 3 gives a rough overview of the preprocessing component used in all subsequently described proposals. We continue with three different proposals for combining machine learning techniques with ontologies (Section 4, viz. document clustering, clustering of content information and discovery of new conceptual relations between concepts. Section 5 explains why ontologies provide suitable means for supporting postprocessing and result presentation and gives several examples. Section 6 concludes with a summary and provides an outlook to future research challenges.

2   OSEM - A Conceptual Architecture for Ontology-Based Text Mining

This section introduces OSEM, a conceptual architecture for using background knowledge in the form of ontologies within text mining. The idea behind OSEM is that a domain- and application-specific ontology acts as a backbone for all phases necessary when applying and using text mining in real-world applications. In general we distinguish the following main phases:

- **Preprocessing and Import & Background Knowledge Provisioning** by User: Includes syntactic preprocessing (shallow linguistic processing including tokenizer, morphology, POS-tagger, etc.) as well as semantic preprocessing (viz. assigning concepts to words, defining conceptual relationships between words). This phase is described in detail in section 3.

- **Mining**: Mining techniques are applied on properly preprocessed data. In general we distinguish between mining on the document level or mining on the object (instance) level. Both approaches take advantage of the ontology as structuring background knowledge. This phase is described in detail in section 4.

- **Postprocessing & Refinement**: Based on the structural backbone of the ontology, results of the text mining algorithm are preprocessed and refined. E.g. the ontology supports in pruning and focusing on specific results of the text mining algorithm. This phase is described in detail in section 5.

- **Presentation**: The postprocessing and refinement phase strongly relates with presentation. Results are presented to the user in an appropriate way, thus, using the ontology as a scaffold for the presentation interfaces.

Figure 1 depicts the overall architecture. We consider as input to the overall process textual documents, structured data and existing ontologies.

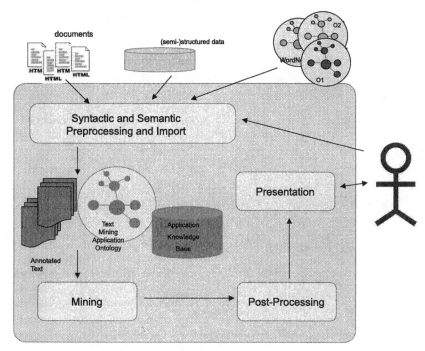

Fig. 1. OSEM Conceptual Architecture

Instantiations of this architecture are described in section 4 focusing on three unsupervised text mining techniques:

- Document clustering

- Instance clustering
- Discovery of conceptual relations

As ontologies play a central in OSEM, we provide in the following a definition of what exactly an ontology is constituted of. Furthermore, we describe how instantiations of ontologies look like and give an example for the relationship between ontologies, instances and textual documents.

Ontologies. In the following we introduce a formal model of our notion of ontologies and associated instances, where a specific focus is set on the interaction of ontology and instances with natural language. To this extend, we have developed a layered architecture. We here only present the part of our overall ontology and instance model that is actually used by OSEM.

Definition 1 (Ontology Layer). An ontology structure is a 6-tupel $\mathcal{O} := \{\mathcal{C}, \mathcal{P}, \mathcal{A}, \mathcal{H}^{\mathcal{C},\mathcal{P}}, prop, att\}$, consisting of three disjoint sets $\mathcal{C}$, $\mathcal{P}$ and $\mathcal{A}$ whose elements are called concept, relation and attribute identifiers, respectively, a **concept hierarchy** $\mathcal{H}^{\mathcal{C}}$: $\mathcal{H}^{\mathcal{C}}$ is a directed relation $\mathcal{H}^{\mathcal{C}} \subseteq \mathcal{C} \times \mathcal{C}$ which is also called taxonomy. $\mathcal{H}^{\mathcal{C}}(C_1, C_2)$ means that C_1 is a sub-concept of C_2, a **function** $prop : \mathcal{P} \to \mathcal{C} \times \mathcal{C}$, that relates concepts non-taxonomically (The function dom: $\mathcal{P} \to \mathcal{C}$ with $\mathrm{dom}(P) := \Pi_1(rel(P))$ gives the domain of P, and range: $\mathcal{P} \to \mathcal{C}$ with $\mathrm{range}(P) := \Pi_2(rel(P))$ give its range. For $prop(P) = (C_1, C_2)$ one may also write $P(C_1, C_2)$). The **relation hierarchy** $\mathcal{H}^{\mathcal{P}}$: $\mathcal{H}^{\mathcal{P}}$ is defined analogously to the concept hierarchy. Thus, a directed relation $\mathcal{H}^{\mathcal{P}} \subseteq \mathcal{P} \times \mathcal{P}$ exists, where $\mathcal{H}^{\mathcal{P}}(P_1, P_2)$ means that P_1 is a sub-relation of P_2. The **function** $att : \mathcal{A} \to \mathcal{C}$ relates concepts with literal values (this means $\mathrm{range}(A) := \mathrm{STRING}$)

As the text mining process typically operates on natural language documents, the core ontology layer presented above is augmented with a lexical layer that facilitates the linking of textual documents to ontological entities.

Definition 2 (Lexical Layer for the Ontology). A lexicon for the core ontology structure $\mathcal{O}$ is a 6-tuple $\mathcal{L} := \{\mathcal{L}^{\mathcal{C}}, \mathcal{L}^{\mathcal{P}}, \mathcal{L}^{\mathcal{A}}, \mathcal{F}, \mathcal{G}, \mathcal{J}\}$ consisting of three sets $\mathcal{L}^{\mathcal{C}}$, $\mathcal{L}^{\mathcal{P}}$ and $\mathcal{L}^{\mathcal{A}}$, whose elements are called **lexical entries** for concepts, relations and attributes, respectively, and three relations $\mathcal{F} \subseteq \mathcal{L}^{\mathcal{C}} \times \mathcal{C}$, $\mathcal{G} \subseteq \mathcal{L}^{\mathcal{P}} \times \mathcal{P}$ and $\mathcal{J} \subseteq \mathcal{L}^{\mathcal{A}} \times \mathcal{A}$ called **references** for concepts, relations and attributes, respectively. Based on $\mathcal{F}$, let for $L \in \mathcal{L}^{\mathcal{C}}$, $\mathcal{F}(L) = \{C \in \mathcal{C} | (L, C) \in \mathcal{F}\}$ and for $\mathcal{F}^{-1}(C) = \{L \in \mathcal{L}^{\mathcal{C}} | (L, C) \in \mathcal{F}\}$. $\mathcal{G}$, $\mathcal{G}^{-1}$, $\mathcal{J}$ and $\mathcal{J}^{-1}$ are defined analogously.

The definition allows n:m-relations between lexical entries and ontological entities, that is a lexical entry may refer to several concepts or relations and one concept or relation may be referenced by several lexical entries.

Definition 3 (Instance Layer). An instance structure is a 6-tuple $\mathcal{MD} :=$ $\{\mathcal{O}, \mathcal{I}, \mathcal{L}, inst, instr, instl\}$, that consists of an ontology $\mathcal{O}$, a set $\mathcal{I}$ whose elements are called instance identifiers (correspondingly C, P and I are disjoint), a set of literal values L, a function $inst : \mathcal{C} \rightarrow 2^{\mathcal{I}}$ called **concept instantiation** (For $inst(C) = I$ one may also write $C(I)$), and a function $instr : \mathcal{P} \rightarrow 2^{\mathcal{I} \times \mathcal{I}}$ called **relation instantiation** (For $instr(P) = \{(I_1, I_2)\}$ one may also write $\{P(I_1, I_2)\}$). The **attribute instantiation** is described via the function $instl : \mathcal{P} \rightarrow 2^{\mathcal{I} \times \mathcal{L}}$ relates instances with literal values. (For $instl(A) = \{(I_1, L)\}$ one may also write $\{A(I_1, L)\}$).

Again, we also define a lexical layer for instances.

Definition 4 (Lexicon for the Instance Structure). A lexicon for the instance structure $\mathcal{KB} := \{\mathcal{O}, \mathcal{I}, inst, instr, instl\}$ is a tuple $\mathcal{L}^{\mathcal{MD}} := (\mathcal{L}^{\mathcal{I}}, \mathcal{J})$ consisting of a set $\mathcal{L}^{\mathcal{I}}$ whose elements are called **lexical entries** for instances, and a relation $\mathcal{J} \subseteq \mathcal{L}^{\mathcal{I}} \times \mathcal{I}$ **reference** for instances, respectively. Based on $\mathcal{J}$, let for $L \in \mathcal{L}^{\mathcal{I}}$, $\mathcal{J}(L) = \{I \in \mathcal{I} | (L, I) \in \mathcal{J}\}$ and for $\mathcal{J}^{-1}(I) = \{L \in \mathcal{L}^{\mathcal{I}} | (L, I) \in \mathcal{J}\}$.

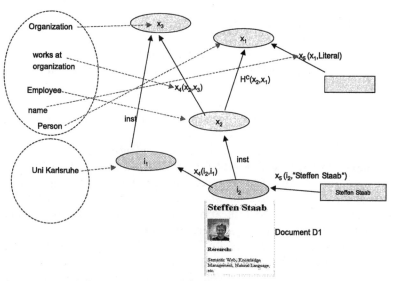

Fig. 2. Example of an instantiated ontology and instance structure

An Example. Let us consider a short example of an instantiated ontology and instance structure as depicted in figure 2. Here $\mathcal{C} := \{x_1, x_2, x_3\}$, $\mathcal{R} := \{x_4\}$, $\mathcal{A} := \{x_5\}$, the relation $x_4(x_1, x_3)$ with its domain/range restrictions and the attribute $x_5(x_2, \text{Literal})$ are defined. The lexical layer is given by $\mathcal{L}^{\mathcal{C}} =$

{ "Organization", "Employee", "Person" }, $\mathcal{L}^{\mathcal{R}}$ = { "works at organization" } and $\mathcal{L}^{\mathcal{A}}$ = { "name" }. $\mathcal{F}$ and $\mathcal{G}$ map the lexical entries to the concepts and relations of the ontology. $\mathcal{F}$ is applied as follows: $\mathcal{F}($ "Organization" $)$ = x_3, $\mathcal{F}($ "Employee" $)$ = x_2, $\mathcal{F}($ "Person" $)$ = x_1, $\mathcal{J}($ "name" $)$ = x_5, and $\mathcal{G}($ "works at organization" $)$ = x_4. Based on this ontology, the following instances may be defined: Assume $\mathcal{I}$:= $\{i_1, i_2\}$. inst is applied as following: inst(i_1) = x_3, inst(i_2) = x_2. The two instances are related by $x_4(i_2, i_1)$, an attribute x_5 for the instance i_2 is defined. Similarly to the lexical entries of concepts and relations the lexical entries of instances may have values, e.g. in this example $\mathcal{L}^{\mathcal{I}}$:= { "Uni Karlsruhe" }. $\mathcal{J}$ is applied as follows: $\mathcal{J}($ "Uni Karlsruhe" $)$ = i_1.

3 Preprocessing Towards a Conceptual Representation

In order to be able to exploit conceptual background knowledge, the preprocessing step requires a conceptual representation of the input texts. For this purpose, we employ a common shallow preprocessing of input texts that maps texts into semantic structures.

3.1 Shallow Syntactic Preprocessing

The mapping of terms to concepts in our approach relies on some modules from third parties, e.g. SMES (Saarbrücken Message Extraction System), a shallow text processor for German (cf. [11]).[2] SMES components we exploit comprise a *tokenizer* based on regular expressions and a *lexical analysis* component including a *word* and a so-called *domain lexicon* (the domain specific part of the lexicon partially defines $\mathcal{F}$).

The tokenizer scans the text in order to identify boundaries of words and complex expressions like "$20.00" or "United States of America", and to expand abbreviations. The word lexicon contains more than 120,000 stem entries. Lexical analysis uses the word lexicon, *(i)*, to perform morphological analysis of terms, i. e. the identification of the canonical common stem of a set of related word forms and the analysis of compounds and, *(ii)*, to recognize named entities. Thus, $\mathcal{L}$ as described in Definition 1 is a set defined by the tokenizer, the word lexicon and the analysis procedures of the lexical analysis component. The domain lexicon contains the mappings from word stems to concepts, i.e. together with the other modules it represents the function $\mathcal{F}$ as defined in Definition 1. By this way, e.g., the expression "Hotel Schwarzer Adler" is associated with the concept HOTEL. During the mapping process we do not resolve ambiguities of terms. This means, if we find several concepts with the same lexical entry we map the term to all related concepts.

---

[2] We also use a simple full form lexicon of our own, which we have derived from WordNet, and GATE [10].

3.2 Concept Vector Representation

Based on the syntactic input, one subsequent text mining variant represents each document as a vector of concept instantiations. Each entry of each vector specifies the frequency that a concept occurs in the document including the frequency that subconcepts occur.

3.3 Instance Representation

Frequently, atomic documents do not constitute the right level of granularity to base the text mining algorithm on. Therefore, as an alternative, we also directly exploit the appearance of instances and their semantic relationships.

In order to derive semantic relationships between instances found in the document we use two strategies:

- Either a finite state machine has the semantic relationship hard-wired into very specific linguistic constructs (e.g. useful for processing of dictionaries).
- Or the establishment of a general syntactic relation triggers the search for a corresponding semantic relation. Background knowledge is then used to check the general availability of such a semantic relationship (cf. [12]).

3.4 A Glimpse onto KAON

Ontologies as well as Vector and instance representations may be stored in RDF and, hence, are accessible through our KAON framework [2] or directly by SQL queries to a proprietary database. The core idea of the common framework is that conceptual structures of different resources (such as different ontology resources) are integrated into a single framework and, thus, easily re-usable for different text mining algorithms. In this sense, we do not explicitly distinguish between data and text mining mechanisms.

4 Mining Component in OSEM

OSEM focuses on the application of unsupervised text mining techniques to the two different data representation layers introduced earlier. In the following section, we first describe a document clustering approach that is based on the usage of a simple, core ontology for generating alternative representations of the given document set such that from the various representations multiple clustering result may be derived by the standard K-Means algorithm. Second, we present an instance clustering approach that takes metadata statements as higher level input for clustering. Third, we present an association rule approach working on the conceptual level using the an ontology at various stage within the mining process.

4.1   Document Clustering

A classical unsupervised text mining task is document clustering. With the abundance of text documents available through the Web or corporate document management systems, the dynamic partitioning of document sets into previously unseen categories ranks high on the priority list for many applications, like business intelligence systems. However, current text clustering approaches tend to neglect several major aspects that greatly limit their practical applicability.

First, text document clustering is mostly seen as an *objective* method, which delivers one clearly defined result, which needs to be "optimal" in some way. This, however, runs contrary to the fact that different people have quite different needs with regard to clustering of texts because they may view the same documents from completely different perspectives (e.g., a business view vs. a technical view). Thus, what is needed are document clustering methods that provide multiple *subjective* perspectives onto the same document set.

Second, text document clustering typically is a machine learning task taking place in a *high-dimensional space* of word vectors, where each word, i.e. each entry of a vector, is seen as a potential attribute for a text. Empirical and mathematical analysis, however, has shown that — in addition to computational inefficiencies — clustering in high-dimensional spaces is very difficult because every data point tends to have the same distance from all other data points (cf. [3]).

Third, text document clustering *per se* is often rather useless, unless it is combined with an *explanation* of why particular texts were categorized into a particular cluster. I.e. one output desired from clustering in practical settings is the explanation of why a particular cluster result was produced besides of the result itself. A common method for producing explanations is the learning of rules based on the cluster results. Again, however, this approach suffers from the high number of features chosen for computing clusters.

Though there are of course different approaches for clustering, simple ones like K-Means or sophisticated ones (like [4]), based on the consideration just mentioned we found that virtually all algorithms working on large feature vectors will eventually face the same principal problems regarding *high-dimensional space* without really approaching the matters of *subjectivity* and *explainability*. Therefore, our objective has been the consideration of different views of the data, i.e. different representations[3] of the same set of text documents, from which alternative clustering results may be derived.

The principal idea of our approach, COSA (Concept Selection and Aggregation), is based on the usage of a simple, core ontology for generating alternative representations of the given document set such that from the various representations multiple clustering result may be derived by the standard K-Means algorithm. The single representations are construed by aggregating

---

[3] Motivated by the database point of view, we also call derived text representations "aggregations".

the original word vector representation in various ways. More precisely, we have compiled a heterarchy of concepts[4]. The heterarchy is navigated top-down by COSA in order to select document features (i.e. concepts) for an aggregated vector representation. Thereby, COSA considers that features are neither too frequent (i.e. COSA would split them into their subconcepts) nor too infrequent (i.e. COSA would abandon them in favor of more frequent ones) to be meaningful for clustering.

Thus, a set of clustering results is produced without interaction by a human user of the system. The user may then decide to prefer the one over the other clustering result based on the actual concepts used for clustering as well as on standard quality measures (such as the silhouette measure [7]).

Let us work through a detailed example to show you the problems and to give you an intuition for the proposed solution. In Table 1 you find a sample of (abbreviated) concept vectors representing the web pages. In Figure 3 one may recognize the corresponding concepts in an excerpt of the ontology. Our simplifying example shows the principal problem of vector representations of documents: The tendency that spurious appearance of concepts (or terms) rather strongly affects the clustering of documents. The reader may bear in mind that our simplification is so extensive that practically it does not appear in such tiny settings, but only when one works with large representations and large document sets. In our simplifying example the appearance of concepts HOTEL, PREMIERE, and CONCERT is spread so evenly across the different documents that all document pairs exhibit (more or less) the same similarity. Corresponding squared Euclidian distances for the example document pairs (1,2), (2,3), (1,3) leads to values of 2, 2, and 2, respectively, and, hence, to no clustering structure at all.

Document #	1 ("Musical")	2 ("Sport Hotel")	3 ("Conference Hotel")
HOTEL	0	1	1
PREMIERE	2	2	1
CONCERT	1	0	1

Table 1. Concept vector representations

When one reduces the size of the representation of our documents, e.g. by projecting into a subspace, one focuses on particular concepts and one may focus on the significant differences that documents exhibit with regard to these concepts. For instance, when we project into a document vector representation that only considers the two dimensions HOTEL and PREMIERE, we will find that document pairs (1,2), (2,3), (1,3) have squared Euclidean distances of 1, 1, and 2. Thus, axis-parallel projections like in this example

---

[4] A heterarchy of concepts is a kind of "taxonomy" where each term may have multiple parents and — of course — multiple children.

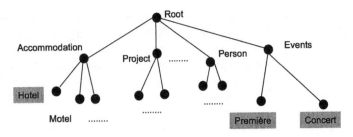

Fig. 3. A sample ontology

may improve the clustering situation. In addition, we may exploit the ontology. For instance, we select features according to the taxonomy, choosing, e.g., EVENTS instead of its subconcepts PREMIERE and CONCERT to built our aggregation. Then, the entries for PREMIERE and CONCERT are added into one vector entry resulting in squared Euclidean distances between pairs (1,2), (2,3), (1,3) of 2, 0, and 2, respectively. Thus, documents 2 and 3 can be clustered together, while document 1 falls into a different cluster.

The algorithm *GenerateConceptViews* described in [6] acts as a preprocessing step for clustering. *GenerateConceptViews* chooses a set of interpretable and ontology-based aggregations leading to modified text representations. Conventional clustering algorithms like K-Means may work on these modified representations producing improved clustering results. Because the size of the vector representation is reduced, it becomes easier for the user to track the decisions made by the clustering algorithms. Because there are a variety of aggregations, the user may choose between alternative clustering results. For instance, there are aggregations such that event pages are clustered together and the rest is set aside or aggregations such that web pages about PREMIERES are clustered together and the rest is left in another cluster. The choice of concepts from the taxonomy thus determines the output of the clustering result and the user may use a view like Figure 3 in order to select and understand differences between clustering results.

4.2   Instance Clustering

In this subsection we present an instance clustering approach that takes instances and instance relations extracted from documents as higher level input for clustering objects. This approach pursues the idea introduced in [5], where information extraction is considered as a preprocessing step before applying text mining. This approach may be more suited for documents containing many links between them or documents that adhere to a fixed structure that is not exploited by the document clustering described algorithm above. In the following we will show exemplary how such a instance structure could be used for the mining step in OSEM.

Measuring Similarity on Ontology-based Instances. As mentioned earlier, clustering of objects requires some kind of similarity measure that is computed between the objects. In our specific case the objects are described via ontology-based instances that serve as input for measuring similarities. Our approach is based on similarities using the instantiated ontology structure and the defined instance structure as introduced earlier in parallel.

Definition 5 (Instance Similarity).

$$sim : (\mathcal{I}, \mathcal{I}) \rightarrow [0, 1]$$

Within the overall similarity computation approach, we distinguish the following three dimensions:

- **Taxonomy Similarity:** Computes the similarity between two instances on the basis of their corresponding concepts and their position in $\mathcal{H}^C$.
- **Relation Similarity:** Compute the similarity between two instances on the basis of their relations to other objects.
- **Attribute Similarity:** Computes the similarity between two instances on the basis of their attributes and attribute values.

Taxonomy Similarity. The taxonomic similarity computed between instances relies on the concepts with their position in the concept taxonomy $\mathcal{H}^C$. The so-called upwards cotopy (SC) is the underlying measure to compute the semantic distance in a concept hierarchy.

Definition 6 (Upwards Cotopy (UC)).

$$UC(C_i, \mathcal{H}^C) := \{C_j \in C | \mathcal{H}^C(C_i, C_j) \vee C_j = C_i\}.$$

The semantic characteristics of $\mathcal{H}^C$ are utilized: The attention is restricted to super-concepts of a given concept C_i and the reflexive relationship of C_i to itself. Based on the definition of the upwards cotopy (UC) the concept match (CM) is then defined:

Definition 7 (Concept Match).

$$CM(C_1, C_2 := \frac{|(UC(C_1, \mathcal{H}^C) \cap (UC(C_2, \mathcal{H}^C))|}{|(UC(C_1, \mathcal{H}^C)) \cup (UC(C_2, \mathcal{H}^C)|}.$$

An Example. A small example is given for computing CM based on a given concept hierarchy $\mathcal{H}^C$. Figure 4 depicts the example scenario graphically. The upwards cotopy $UC(CHRISTIANISM, \mathcal{H}^C)$ is given by

$$(UC(((\{CHISTIANISM\}), \mathcal{H}^C)) = \{CHRISTIANISM, RELIGION, ROOT\}.$$

The upwards cotopy $UC((\{MUSLIM\}), \mathcal{H}^C)$ is computed by

$$UC(((\{MUSLIM\}), \mathcal{H}^C) = \{MUSLIM, RELIGION, ROOT\}.$$

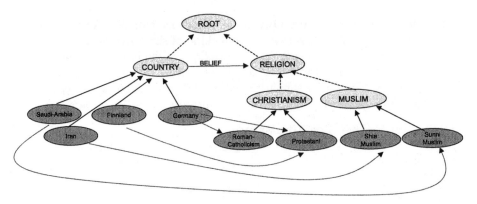

Fig. 4. Example for computing similarities

Based on the upwards cotopy one can compute the concept match CM between two given specific concepts. The concept match CM between MUSLIM and CHRISTIANISM is given as $\frac{1}{2}$.

Definition 8 (Taxonomy Similarity).

$$\text{TS}(I_1, I_2) = \begin{cases} 1 & \text{if } I_1 = I_2 \\ \frac{CM(C(I_1), C(I_2))}{2} & \text{otherwise} \end{cases}$$

Thus, the taxonomy similarity between SHIA MUSLIM to PROTESTANT is $\frac{1}{4}$.

Relation Similarity. It is pretty save to assume that if two instances have the same relation to a third instance, they are more likely similar than two instances that have relations to totally different instances. We incorporated this observation into our algorithm by changing the similarity of two instances depending on the similarity of the instances they have relations to. The similarity of the referred instances is once again calculated using taxonomic similarity. For example, assuming we are given two concepts COUNTRY and RELIGION and a relation BELIEVE(COUNTRY, RELIGION). The algorithm will infer that specific countries believing in catholicism and protestantism are more similar than either of these two compared to Hinduism because more countries have both catholics and protestants than a combination of either of these and hindus.

After this overview, let's get to the nitty gritty of really defining the similarity on relations. We are comparing two instances I_1 and I_2, $I_1, I_2 \in \mathcal{I}$. From the definition of the ontology we know that there is a set of relations P_1 that allow instance I_1 either as domain, as range or both (Likewise there is a set P_2 for I_2). Only the intersection $P_{CO} = P_1 \cap P_2$ will be of interest for relation similarity because differences between P_1 and P_2 are determined by the taxonomic relations, which are already taken into account by the taxonomic similarity.

The set P_{CO} of relations is differentiated between relations allowing I_1 and I_2 as range - P_{co-I}, and those that allow I_1 and I_2 as domain - P_{co-O}.

Definition 9 (Incoming P_{co-I} and Outgoing P_{co-O} Relations). for an ontology $\mathcal{O} := \{\mathcal{C}, \mathcal{P}, \mathcal{A}, \mathcal{H}^{C,P}, prop, att\}$ and instances I_i and I_j let

$$H^{trans} := \{(a,b) : (\exists a_1 ... a_n \in C : H^C(a, a_1) ... H^C(a_n, b))\}$$

$$P_{co-Ii}(I_i) := \{R : R \in \mathcal{P} \land ((C(I_i), range(R)) \in H^{trans})\}$$

$$P_{co-Oi}(I_i) := \{R : R \in \mathcal{P} \land ((C(I_i), domain(R)) \in H^{trans})\}$$

$$P_{co-I}(I_i, I_j) := P_{co-Ii}(I_i) \cap P_{co-I}(I_j)$$

$$P_{co-O}(I_i, I_j) := P_{co-Oi}(I_i) \cap P_{co-O}(I_j)$$

In the following we will only look at P_{co-O}, but everything applies to P_{co-I} as well. Before we continue we have to note an interesting aspect: For a given ontology with a relation P_x there is a minimum similarity greater than zero between any two instances that are source or target of an instance relation - $MinSim_{s(P_x)}$ and $MinSim_{t(P_x)}$[5]. Ignoring this will increase the similarity of two instances with relations to the most different instances when compared to two instances that simply don't define this relation. This is especially troublesome when dealing with missing values.

For each relation $P_n \in P_{co-O}$ and each instance I_i there exists a set of instance relations $P_n(I_i, I_x)$. We will call the set of instances I_x the associated instances A_s.

Definition 10 (Associated Instances).

$$A_s(P, I) := \{I_x : I_x \in \mathcal{I} \land P(I, I_x)\}$$

The task of comparing the instances I_1 and I_2 with respect to relation P_n boils down to comparing $A_s(P_n, I_1)$ with $A_s(P_n, I_2)$. This is done as follows:

Definition 11 (Similarity for one Relation).

$$OR(I_1, I_2, P) = \begin{cases} MinSim_{t(P)} & \text{if } A_s(P, I_1) = \emptyset \lor A_s(P, I_2) = \emptyset \\ \left(\dfrac{\sum_{(a \in A_s(P, I_1))} \max\{sim(a,b) | b \in A_s(P, I_2)\}}{|A_s(P, I_1)|} \right) & \text{if } |A_s(P, I_1)| \geq |A_s(P, I_2)| \\ \left(\dfrac{\sum_{(a \in A_s(P, I_2))} \max\{sim(a,b) | b \in A_s(P, I_1)\}}{|A_s(P, I_2)|} \right) & \text{otherwise} \end{cases}$$

Finally, the results for all $P_n \in P_{co-O}$ and $P_n \in P_{co-I}$ are combined by calculating their arithmetic mean.

---

[5] Range and domain specify a concept and any two instances of this concept or one of its sub-concepts will have a taxonomic similarity bigger than zero

Definition 12 (Relational Similarity).

$$RS(I_1, I_2) := \frac{\sum_{p \in P_{\text{co-I}}} \text{OR}(I_1, I_2, p) + \sum_{p \in P_{\text{co-O}}} \text{OR}(I_1, I_2, p)}{|P_{\text{co-I}}| + |P_{\text{co-O}}|}$$

The last problem that remains is the recursive nature of process of calculating similarities that may lead to infinite cycles, but it can be easily solved by imposing a maximum depth for the recursion. After reaching this maximum depth the arithmetic mean of taxonomic and attribute similarity is returned.

Example. Figure 3 gives an ontology and a set of instance instances that we can use for an example of relational similarity. Assuming we compare FINLAND and GERMANY, we see that the set of common relations only contains the BELIEF relation. As the next step we compare the sets of instances associated with GERMANY and FINLAND through the belief relation - that's {ROMAN-CATHOLICISM, PROTESTANT} for GERMANY and PROTESTANT for FINNLAND. The similarity function for PROTESTANT compared with PROTESTANT returns one because they are equal, but the similarity of PROTESTANT compared with ROMAN-CATHOLICISM once again depends on their relational similarity.

If we we assume the the maximum depth of recursion is set to one, the relational similarity between ROMAN-CATHOLICISM and PROTESTANT is 0.5^6. So finally the relational similarity between^{Finnland} and GERMANY in this example is 0.75.

Attribute Similarity. Attribute similarity focuses on similar attribute values to infer the similarity between two instances. As attributes are very similar to relations, most of what is said for relations also applies here.

Definition 13 (Compared Attributes for two Instances).

$$P_A i(I_i) := \{A : A \in \mathcal{A} \wedge A(I_i, L_x)\}$$

$$P_A(I_i, I_j) := P_A i(I_i) \cap P_A i(I_j)$$

Definition 14 (Attribute Values).

$$A_s(A, I_i) := \{L_x : L_x \in \mathcal{L} \wedge A(I_i, L_x)\}$$

Only the members of the sets A_s defined earlier are not instances but literals and we need a new similarity method to compare literals. Because attributes can be names, date of birth, population of a country, income etc. comparing them in a senseful way is very difficult. We decided to try to parse

---

[6] The set of associated instances for PROTESTANT contains FINLAND and GERMANY, the set for ROMAN-CATHOLICISM just GERMANY.

the attribute values as a known data type (so far only date or number)[7] and to do the comparison on the parsed values. If it's not possible to parse all values of a specific attribute, we ignore this attribute. But even if numbers are compared, translating a numeric difference to a similarity value $[0, 1]$ can be difficult. For example comparing the attribute population of a country a difference of 4 should yield a similarity value very close to 1, but comparing the attribute "average number of children per woman" the same numeric difference value should result in a similarity value close to 0. To take this into account, we first find the maximum difference between values of this attribute and then calculate the the similarity as $1 - (\text{Difference}/\max \text{Difference})$.

Definition 15 (Literal Similarity).

$$slsim(\mathcal{A}, \mathcal{A}) \to [0, 1]$$

$$mlsim := \max \left\{ slsim(A_1, A_2) : A_1 \in \mathcal{A} \wedge A_2 \in \mathcal{A} \right\}$$

$$lsim(A_i, A_j, A) := \frac{slsim(A_i, A_j)}{mlsim(A)}$$

And last but not least, unlike for relations the minimal similarity when comparing attributes is always zero.

Definition 16 (Similarity for one Attribute).

$$OA(I_1, I_2, A) := \begin{cases} 0 & \text{if } A_s(A, I_1) = \emptyset \vee A_s(A, I_2) = \emptyset \\ \left(\dfrac{\sum_{(a \in A_s(A, I_1))} \max\{lsim(a,b,A)|b \in A_s(A, I_2)\}}{|A_s(A, I_1)|} \right) & \text{if } |A_s(A, I_1)| \geq |A_s(A, I_2)| \\ \left(\dfrac{\sum_{(a \in A_s(A, I_2))} \max\{lsim(a,b,A)|b \in A_s(A, I_1)\}}{|A_s(A, I_2)|} \right) & \text{otherwise} \end{cases}$$

Definition 17 (Attribute Similarity).

$$AS(I_1, I_2) := \frac{\sum_{a \in P_{\mathrm{A}}(I_1, I_2)} OA(I_1, I_2, a)}{|P_{\mathrm{A}(I_1, I_2)}|}$$

---

[7] For simple string data types one may use a notion of string similarity: The *edit distance* formulated by Levenshtein [8] is a well-established method for weighting the difference between two strings. It measures the minimum number of token insertions, deletions, and substitutions required to transform one string into another using a dynamic programming algorithm. For example, the edit distance, ed, between the two lexical entries *TopHotel* and *Top_Hotel* equals 1, ed(*TopHotel*, *Top_Hotel*) = 1, because one insertion operation changes the string "TopHotel" into "Top_Hotel".

Combined Measure. The combined measure uses the three dimensions introduced above in a common measure. This is done by calculating the weighted arithmetic mean of attribute, relation and semantic similarity.

Definition 18 (Similarity Measure).

$$sim(I_i, I_j) := \frac{t \times TS(I_i, I_j) + r \times RS(I_i, I_j) + a \times AS(I_i, I_j)}{t + r + a}$$

The weights may be adjusted according to the given data set the measures should be applied on, e.g. within our empirical evaluation we used a weight of 2 for relation similarity, because most of the overall information of the ontology and the associated instance was contained in the relations.

The similarity measures introduced above allow to compute similarities between a set of instances. We consider this step as a specific form of pre-processing to generate a similarity matrix that may serve as input for a hierarchical clustering algorithm, e.g. as described in [9].

Empirical Evaluation. We have empirically evaluated our approach for clustering ontology-based instances based on the different similarity measures and the clustering algorithm introduced above. We used the well-known CIA world fact book data set as input[8]. The data set is available in many different forms as MONDIAL databases[9]. Due to a lack of currently available ontology-based instance on the Web, we converted a subset of MONDIAL in RDF and modeled a corresponding RDF-Schema for the databases (on the basis of the ER model also provided by MONDIAL). It has to be noted that the MONDIAL database has a lot of missing and even wrong values. Our subset of the MONDIAL database contained the concepts COUNTRY, LANGUAGE, ETHNIC-GROUP, RELIGION and CONTINENT. Relations contained where

- SPEAK(COUNTRY,LANGUAGE),
- BELONG(COUNTRY, ETHNIC-GROUP),
- BELIEVE(COUNTRY,RELIGION),
- BORDERS(COUNTRY,COUNTRY) and
- ENCOMPASSES(COUNTRY,CONTINENT).

We also converted the attributes infant mortality and population growth of the concept COUNTRY.

The task was now to calculate the hierarchical cluster structure for countries using the data set introduced above. As there is no pre-classification of

---

[8] http://www.cia.gov/cia/publications/factbook/
[9] http://www.informatik.uni-freiburg.de/ may/Mondial/

countries, we decided to empirically evaluate the cluster against the country clusters we know and use in our daily live (like European countries, scandinavian countries, arabic countries etc). Sadly there is no further taxonomic information for the concepts RELIGION, ETHNIC–GROUP or LANGUAGE available within the data set. Thus, the taxonomic similarity measure could not be applied within this evaluation study. We first feed the clustering algorithm with a similarity matrix that has been generated using only relation similarity measures, than with a similarity matrix that has been generated using only attribute similarity measures and finally with a similarity matrix using a the combined relational and attribute similarity measure. For our experiments we used the already introduced bottom-up clustering algorithm with a single linkage computation strategy using cosine measure.

Using only Relation Similarity. Using only the relations of countries for measuring similarities we got clusters resembling many real world country clusters, like the European countries, the former Soviet republics in the caucasus or such small cluster like {AUSTRIA, GERMANY}. A particular interesting example is the cluster of scandinavian countries depicted in Figure 5 because our data nowhere contains a value like "scandinavian language" or a ethnic group "scandinavian".[10]

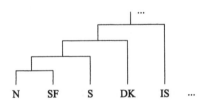

Fig. 5. Example clustering result – Scandinavian countries

Figure 6 shows another interesting cluster of countries that we know as the Middle East[11]. The politically interested reader will immediately recognize that Israel is missing. This can be easily explained by observing that Israel, while geographically in the middle east is in terms of language, religion and ethnic group a very different country. More troublesome is that Oman is missing too and this can be only explained by turning to the data set used to calculate the similarities, where we see that Oman is missing many values, for example any relation to language or ethnic group.

---

[10] The meaning of the acronyms in the picture is: N:Norway, SF: Finnland, S: Sweden, DK: Denmark and IS:Island.

[11] The meaning of the acronyms used in the picture is: Q:Quatar, KWT: Kuwait, UAE: United Arab Emirates, SA: Saudi Arabia, JOR: Jordan, RL: Lebanon, IRQ: Iraq, SYR: Syria, YE, Yemen.

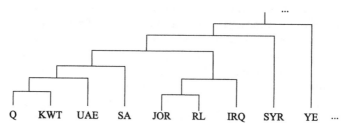

Fig. 6. Example clustering result – Middle East

Using only Attribute Similarity. When using only attributes of countries for measuring similarities we had to restrict the clustering to infant mortality and population growth. As infant mortality and population growth are good indicators for wealth of a country, we got cluster like industrialized countries or very poor countries.

Combining Relation and Attribute Similarity. At first surprisingly the clusters generated with the combination of attribute and relation similarity closely resemble the clusters generated only with relation similarity. But after checking the attribute values of the countries it actually increased our confidence in the algorithm, because countries that are geographically close together, and are similar in terms of ethnic group, religion and language are almost always also similar in terms of population growth and infant mortality. In the few cases where this was not the case the countries where rated far apart, for example Saudi Arabia and Iraq lost it's position in the core middle east cluster depicted because of their high infant mortality[12].

Summarization of Results. Due to the lack of pre-classified countries and due to the subjectivity of clustering in general, we had to restrict our evaluation procedure to an empirical evaluation of the cluster we obtained against the country clusters we know and use in our daily live. It has been seen that using our attribute and relation similarity measures combined with a hierarchical clustering algorithm results in reasonable clusters of countries taking into account the very different aspects a country may be described and classified.

4.3 Association Rules

Association rules have been established in the area of data mining, thus, finding interesting association relationships among a large set of data items. Many

---

[12] It may be surprising for such a rich country, but according to the CIA world fact book the infant mortality rate in Saudi Arabia (51 death per 1000 live born children) much closer resembles that of sanctioned Iraq (60) than that of much poorer countries like Syria (33) or Lebanon (28)

industries become interested in mining association rules from their databases (e.g. for helping in many business decisions such as customer relationship management, cross-marketing and loss-leader analysis. A typical example of association rule mining is market basket analysis. This process analyzes customer buying habits by finding associations between the different items that customers place in their shopping baskets. The information discovered by association rules may help to develop marketing strategies, e.g. layout optimization in supermarkets (placing milk and bread within close proximity may further encourage the sale of these items together within single visits to the store). In [1] concrete examples for extracted associations between items are given. The examples are based supermarket products that are included in a set of transactions collected from customers' purchases. One of the classical association rule that has been extracted from these databases is that "diaper are purchased together with beer".

For the purpose of illustration, an example is provided to the reader. The example is based on actual experiments. A text corpus given by a WWW provider for tourist information has been processed. The corpus describes actual objects referring to locations, accommodations, furnishings of accommodations, administrative information, or cultural events, such as given in the following example sentences.

(1) a. "Mecklenburg's" schönstes HOTEL liegt in Rostock. ("Mecklenburg's" most beautiful hotel is located in Rostock.)

 b. Ein besonderer Service für unsere Gäste ist der "Frisörsalon" in unserem Hotel. (A "hairdresser" in our "hotel" is a special service for our guests.)

 c. Das Hotel Mercure hat "Balkone" mit direktem "Strandzugang". (The hotel Mercure offers "balconies" with direct "access" to the beach.)

 d. Alle "Zimmer" sind mit "TV", Telefon, Modem und Minibar ausgestattet. (All "rooms" have "TV", telephone, modem and minibar.)

Processing the example sentences (1a) and (1b) the dependency relations between the lexical entries are extracted (and some more). In sentences (1c) and (1d) the heuristic for prepositional phrase-attachment and the sentence heuristic relate pairs of lexical entries, respectively. Thus, four concept pairs – among many others – are derived with knowledge from the lexicon.

Table 2. Examples for linguistically related pairs of concepts

L_1	$a_{i,1}$	L_2	$a_{i,2}$
"Mecklenburg's"	AREA	*hotel*	HOTEL
"hairdresser"	HAIRDRESSER	*hotel*	HOTEL
"balconies"	BALCONY	*access*	ACCESS
"room"	ROOM	*TV*	TELEVISION

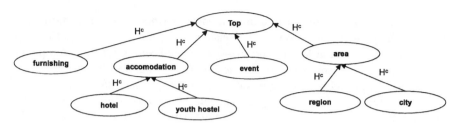

Fig. 7. An example concept taxonomy as background knowledge for non-taxonomic relation extraction

The algorithm for learning generalized association rules uses the concept hierarchy, an excerpt of which is depicted in Figure 7, and the concept pairs from above (among many other concept pairs). In our actual experiments, it discovered a large number of interesting and important non-taxonomic conceptual relations. A few of them are listed in Table 3. Note that in this table we also list two conceptual pairs, viz. (AREA, HOTEL) and (ROOM, TELEVISION), that are not presented to the user, but that are pruned. The reason is that there are ancestral association rules, viz. (AREA, ACCOMMODATION) and (ROOM, FURNISHING), respectively with higher confidence and support measures.

Table 3. Examples of discovered non-taxonomic relations

Discovered relation	Confidence	Support
(AREA, ACCOMMODATION)	0.38	0.04
~~(AREA, HOTEL)~~	~~0.1~~	~~0.03~~
(ROOM, FURNISHING)	0.39	0.03
~~(ROOM, TELEVISION)~~	~~0.29~~	~~0.02~~
(ACCOMMODATION, ADDRESS)	0.34	0.05
(RESTAURANT, ACCOMMODATION)	0.33	0.02

5   Postprocessing and Presentation

Even without background knowledge a major component of unsupervised Text Mining is the postprocessing and presentation component. The reasons essentially are that

- No algorithm can reliably predict what is novel, interesting and useful;
- The results are typically so complex that they cannot be represented in a short phrase or formula or a small picture;
- Even fairly understandable results must be made digestible for a more naive user who is typically not an expert in statistics or data mining, but has an application background.

Background knowledge *per se* does not diminish any of these three problems. However, ontologies add one (or several) additional dimensions that allow the user to explore the results in a way that corresponds to his way of thinking in the application domain. For instance, in the skill management scenario it is not very intuitive for the naive user to think in terms of distance to a hyperplane in some high-dimensional space, but it is quite easy for him to understand an explanation that says "these two clusters are the same on all attributes, but this group of people also has foreign language skills".

Techniques. Technically speaking, this sort of explanation is realized by some core means:[13]

- Navigation. Either navigation in the ontology may be used to select data mining results or data mining results may be selected in order to focus on some ontology parts.
- Exploiting hierarchical relationships of an ontology, e.g. the taxonomic relation $\mathcal{H}^C$ or some part-whole hierarchy (e.g., car-body being part of a car). Different results may be sorted according to the branching of attribute values into different parts of such a hierarchy. In addition, several dimensions may be constructed from such attribute values resulting in a lattice of different results.
- Focusing on the parts of the ontology that best explain a particular result. For instance, when clustering concept vectors one finds that not all vector entries are of similar value for producing the final clustering results. Thus, the explanation can be focused to focal parts of the ontology. At the same time hierarchies in the ontology may be split or aggregated depending on which view is more promising to the user who explores the result.

While we have expanded only on a few mechanisms (e.g., navigation, zooming into particular concepts, selection of data mining results), there is plenty of work in visualizing ontologies and corresponding database entries that may be reused for visualizing knowledgeable text mining results.[14]

6 Conclusion

Text Mining is about discovering novel, interesting and useful patterns from textual data. In this paper we have discussed several means that introduce background knowledge into unsupervised text mining in order to improve the novelty, the interestingness or the usefulness of the detected patterns. Germane to the different proposals is that they strive for higher abstractions that carry more explanatory power and more possibilities for exploring the input texts than is achievable by unknowledgeable means.

---

[13] The means, of course, depend to some extent on the data mining techniques exploited.

[14] Cf. http://www.aidministrator.nl for some commercial tools.

Acknowledgments

The research presented in this paper has been partially funded by DaimlerChrysler AG, Woerth in the HRMore project and by Deutsche Telekom AG.

References

1. R. Agrawal, T. Imielinski, and A. Swami. Mining Associations between Sets of Items in Massive Databases. In *Proceedings of the 1993 ACM SIGMOD International Conference on Management of Data, Washington, D.C., May 26-28, 1993*, pages 688–692. ACM Press, 1993.
2. Alexander Maedche, Steffen Staab, Rudi Studer, York Sure, and Raphael Volz. Seal - tying up information integration and web site management by ontologies. In *IEEE Data Engineering Bulletin*, volume 25, March 2002.
3. K. Beyer, J. Goldstein, R. Ramakrishnan, and U. Shaft. When is 'nearest neighbor' meaningful. In *Proc. of ICDT-1999*, pages 217–235, 1999.
4. P. Bradley, U. Fayyad, and C. Reina. Scaling clustering algorithms to large databases. In *Proc. of KDD-1998*, pages 9–15. AAAI Press, August 1998.
5. Ronen Feldman, Yonatan Aumann, Moshe Fresko, Orly Lipshtat, Binyamin Rosenfeld, and Yonatan Schler. Text mining via information extraction. In *Proceedings of PKDD-99, Prague, 1999*. Springer, 1999.
6. A. Hotho, A. Maedche, and S. Staab. Ontology-based text clustering. In *Proceedings of the IJCAI-2001 Workshop "Text Learning: Beyond Supervision", August, Seattle, USA*, 2001.
7. L. Kaufman and P.J. Rousseeuw. *Finding Groups in Data: An Introduction to Cluster Analysis*. Wiley, New York, 1990.
8. I. V. Levenshtein. Binary Codes capable of correcting deletions, insertions, and reversals. *Cybernetics and Control Theory*, 10(8):707–710, 1966.
9. C.D. Manning and H. Schuetze. *Foundations of Statistical Natural Language Processing*. MIT Press, Cambridge, Massachusetts, 1999.
10. D. Maynard, V. Tablan, H. Cunningham, C. Ursu, H. Saggion, K. Bontcheva, and Y. Wilks. Architectural elements of language engineering robustness. *Journal of Natural Language Engineering – Special Issue on Robust Methods in Analysis of Natural Language Data*, 2002.
11. G. Neumann, R. Backofen, J. Baur, M. Becker, and C. Braun. An information extraction core system for real world german text processing. In *In Proceedings of ANLP-97*, pages 208–215, Washington, USA, 1997.
12. S. Staab, C. Braun, A. Düsterhöft, A. Heuer, M. Klettke, S. Melzig, G. Neumann, B. Prager, J. Pretzel, H.-P. Schnurr, R. Studer, H. Uszkoreit, and B. Wrenger. GETESS — searching the web exploiting german texts. In *CIA'99 — Proceedings of the 3rd Workshop on Cooperative Information Agents. Upsala, Sweden, July 31-August 2, 1999*, LNCS 1652, pages 113–124, Berlin, 1999. Springer.

Using Adaptive Information Extraction for Effective Human-Centred Document Annotation

Fabio Ciravegna[1], Alexiei Dingli[1], Yorick Wilks[1], and Daniela Petrelli[2]

[1] Department of Computer Science, University of Sheffield, Regent Court,
211 Portobello Street, Sheffield S1 4DP
{fabio, alexiei, yorick}@dcs.shef.ac.uk
[2] Department of Information Studies, University of Sheffield, Regent Court,
211 Portobello Street, Sheffield S1 4DP
d.petrelli@shef.ac.uk

Abstract. In this paper we propose a methodology for supporting human-centred annotation of documents, based on adaptive information extraction. We describe the interplay between IE system, annotation interface and users. We discuss our model in terms of timeliness and intrusiveness of the IE system with respect to the human activity. Then we present an experiment that quantifies the gain in using IE as support to human annotators.

1 Introduction

Text annotation is a way for structuring documents so to allow accessing knowledge instead of unstructured material. Fields such as the Semantic Web (SW) and Knowledge Management (KM) need text annotation e.g., for document indexing or for the population of ontologies with instances extracted from documents. Unfortunately human annotation is a slow time-consuming process that involves high costs and therefore it is vital for these fields to produce efficient and effective annotation possibly using automatic or semi-automatic methods. Information Extraction Systems (IES) are the perfect support for documents annotation as they can work either in an unsupervised way (automatic annotation of documents) or semi-automatic way (e.g. as support for human annotators). For the successful application of IE in fields such as SW and KM it is necessary that IE systems are easily portable to new applications without any knowledge of NLP or IE, in principle using only the description of the domain (e.g. the ontology) and a corpus of annotated texts [6]. The IE research community has spent a big effort in the last years on the application of Machine Learning to IE [4]. IES adaptable using just the domain description and an annotated training corpus are now available [3], [1], [5]. As result, some tools for the SW and KM have started including adaptive IE capabilities as support for annotation [11], [14]. In such systems the ontology describing the domain is used to derive the IES tagset. Then the user starts annotating the corpus using a graphical interface;

the IES monitors such annotations and learns how to reproduce them; when equivalent cases are found in other documents, annotations are automatically added by the IE system and presented to the user for revision. These integrations of IES and annotation interfaces are very preliminary and still largely to be refined. Moreover there is the need to actually demonstrate the degree of effectiveness of the IE-based annotation tools, beyond the simple intuition of usefulness.

In this paper we propose a methodology of interaction among users, annotation interface and IE system that maximises the cooperation among the three in order to obtain reliable annotation with minimum effort. We also present the results of experiments that demonstrate the effectiveness and usefulness of IE-based document annotations. Finally we discuss some open issues on the use of IE for annotation.

2   Desiderata for IE-Based Annotation

We define two user-centred criteria as measure of appropriateness for the IE-based support to human annotators: *timeliness* and *intrusiveness*. The first shows the ability to react to user annotation. The latter represents the level to which the IES bothers the user.

Timeliness: When the IES is trained on blocks of texts (as in most of the current annotation systems), there is a gap between the moment in which the user inserts annotations and the moment in which the system learns from them. If a batch of texts contains many similar documents, users spend time in annotating them without any help from the IES, for the simple reason that no learning session is scheduled for the moment. The IES is not supportive, neither is the user effort very useful for the IES since very similar cases do not offer the variety of phenomena that empower learning. The bigger the size of the batch of texts the worse the problem is.

Intrusiveness: In the current interfaces it is difficult to avoid bothering users with annotations generated by unreliable rules (e.g. induced using an insufficient number of cases). This problem is mainly related to the tuning of the IES behaviour. Some IES provide internal tuning methods (e.g. rule error thresholds tuning), but such methods are generally unsuitable for naive users, as they require knowledge of the underlying IE system. A user-friendly interaction methodology is needed to help selecting the appropriate level of proactivity (as opposed to intrusiveness), without requiring users to cope with the complexity of tuning an IES. Another level of intrusiveness is given by the training time required by the IES. This can take a considerable amount of CPU time and therefore it can stop the annotation session for a while. A positive collaboration requires not to constraint the user time to the IES training time.

3   Interaction Model

The proposed interaction model aims at providing non-intrusive and timely active annotation. The first constraint for non-intrusiveness is that the IES must not impose any specific methodology of annotation or any specific adaptation on users. It must integrate in the usual user environment and the interaction with users must be left to the annotation interface, a tool specifically designed to interact with annotators in a proper way. In this model, IE is a service to the interface, not to users. Users will just notice that at some point annotations are suggested by the interface and they can even ignore that an IES is producing such annotation.

The annotation process is split in two main phases from the IES point of view:

(1) **training** and
(2) **active annotation with revision**.

In user terms the first corresponds to unassisted annotation, while the latter just requires correction or integration of proposed annotation, as explained in the rest of the section.

In describing our model we hypothesize the case of a typical annotation interface (e.g., [10], [9]), where relevant portions of text are selected using the mouse and then annotation are inserted selecting from a list. Different colours are associated to different tags and inserted annotations are highlighted using such colour code. The methodology described in the rest of the section was implemented in Melita, an annotation interface specifically designed for the SW and KM, using a mouse-based annotation approach. Melita uses Amilcare, an implementation of the $(LP)^2$ algorithm [8], as supporting IES.

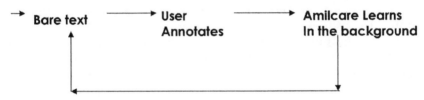

Fig. 1. Bootstrapping where the IES (Amilcare)learns in the background

3.1   Training

During training users annotate texts without any contribution from the IES. We define two sub-phases: *bootstrapping* and *training with verification*. In bootstrapping the only IES task is to learn in the background from the user annotations (figure 1). The duration of bootstrapping depends on the specific IES requirements, e.g., on the minimum number of examples needed for a minimum training (ideally just one text).

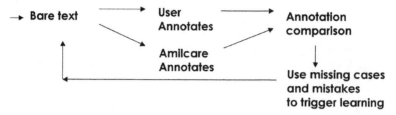

Fig. 2. Training with verification: the IES learns and tests in the background

During *training with verification* (figure 2), the unassisted annotation continues, but the behaviour of the IES changes. The IES silently competes with the user in annotating the document, comparing its hypotheses with the user annotations and using missed and wrong matches to retrain its learner. The training phase ends when the accuracy in annotating can provide the user preferred level of proactivity and therefore it is possible to move to *active annotation*. We will discuss in the following how this condition is verified.

3.2   Active Annotation with Revision

The annotation process is here heavily based on suggestions from the IES (figure 3). The user task is mainly correcting and integrating the suggested annotations (i.e. remove or add annotations). Human corrections and integrations are inputted back to the IES for retraining. The real system-user cooperation takes place here: the system helps the user in annotating; the user provides feedback to help the system perform better. In user terms this is where the added value of the IES becomes apparent, because it heavily reduces the amount of work the user has to do. It is easy to see that correcting annotations is simpler and less time consuming than annotating bare texts.

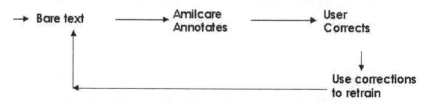

Fig. 3. Active annotation: the IES proposes annotations and learns from user feedback

Notice that the interface can be in different statuses for different annotation types at the same type: this is because - as we will see in section 4 - some types of annotations are easy to learn and therefore the IES is ready for active annotation after limited training, while for other information more training is needed. From the user point of view this is irrelevant, as they will just notice that at some point suggestions are provided for some types of information and not for others. In section 4.1 we will present some experiments showing how fast a system can move from bootstrapping to active annotation.

3.3   Intrusiveness versus Proactivity

Intrusiveness is the risk related to active annotation. On the one hand when the system suggests annotations, it can bother users with unreliable suggestions. The requirement here is to enable users to tune the IES behaviour so that the reliability of suggestions is appropriate. The interface must bridge the qualitative vision of users (e.g. "be more/less active/accurate") with specific IES settings (e.g. change error thresholds). In our implementation a number of IES settings are manually associated to specific interface settings. This means that users manipulate concepts such as recall and precision and the interface modifies the IES settings accordingly. In practice Melita's settings influence the selection of rules in Amilcare at training time by tuning requirements on maximum acceptable error rate, minimum number of covered cases and even the way in which rule generalization is performed (more or less aggressive).

3.4   Just in Time Learning

IES training requires CPU time, thus slowing down or even stopping the user activity. Most systems use batch training to limit the user's waiting time, but - as mentioned - the batch approach presents timeliness problems. We propose a scheduling of activities both allowing timeliness in learning and limiting the user idle time. Instead of stopping the user activity for training the IES, we perform training while the user annotate texts. In principle it would be possible to treat every annotation event in the interface as a request to train on a specific example, but this requires the ability to retreat annotations in case of user mistakes, making the interaction with the IES quite complex. In our model when a document is opened the IES provides the support using rules induced from the annotated corpus but the last document. While the user annotates the current document (e.g. correcting imprecision) the IES trains on the last saved document. Here timeliness is only partially guaranteed, because the IES annotation capability always refers to rules learned by using the entire annotated corpus but the last document. This means that the IES is not able to help when two similar documents are annotated in sequence, like in training in batches of two documents. The advantage is that there is no idle time for the user, as the manual annotation of a document generally requires a great deal more time than training on a single text. Actually timeliness is a matter of perception: the only important matter - we believe - is that users perceive it. Considering that in many applications the order in which documents are annotated is irrelevant, it is possible to organize annotation so to both avoid presenting similar documents in sequence and hide the small lack of timeliness. A simple measure of similarity of texts from the annotation point of view is sufficient here: at the end of each learning session the induced rules are applied to the unannotated part of the corpus. The number of matches on each text is used as an approximation of similarity among texts: equivalent inserted annotations mean similarity; different inserted annotations mean actual difference. We always present users with sequences of documents to be annotated where adjacent texts are classified as dissimilar from the available rules. This is sufficient to avoid the user perception of lack of timeliness. As we will see in the following this strategy also improves the IES effectiveness.

4 Evaluating IE's Effectiveness

We performed a number of experiments for demonstrating how fast the IES can converge to an active annotation status and to quantify its contribution to the annotation task, i.e. its ability to suggest correctly. We selected the CMU seminar announcements corpus, where 483 emails are manually annotated with speaker, starting time, ending time and location of seminars [12]. Such corpus was already used for evaluating a number of adaptive algorithms [12], [2], [13], [7], [15]. In our experiment the annotation in the corpus was used to simulate human annotation in the methodology described above. We have evaluated the potential contribution of the IE system at regular intervals during corpus tagging, i.e. after the annotation of 5, 10, 20, 25, 30, 50, 62, 75, 100 and 150 documents (each subset fully including the previous one). Each time we tested the accuracy of the IES on the following 200 texts in the corpus (so when training on 25 texts, the test was performed also on the following 25 texts that will be used for training on 50). The ability to suggest on the test corpus was measured in terms of precision and recall. Recall represents here an approximation of the probability that the user receives a suggestion in tagging a new document. Precision represents the probability that such suggestion is correct. Results are shown in figure 4. On the X-axis the number of documents provided for training is shown. On the Y-axis precision, recall and f-measure[1] are presented. The maximum gain comes in annotating stime and etime. This is not surprising as they present quite regular fillers. After training on only 20 texts, the system is potentially able

---

[1] A balanced average of precision and recall.

to propose 368 stimes (out of 491), 303 are correct, 18 partially correct[2], 47 wrong, leading to Precision=84 Recall=61. With 30 texts the recognition reaches P=91, R=78, with 50 P=92, R=80. The situation is very similar for etime, while it is more complex for speaker and location, where 80% f-measure is reached only after about 100 texts. This is due to the fact that locations and speakers are much more difficult to learn than time expressions because they are much less regular. We performed the same type of analysis on other corpora such as the Austin TX Jobs announcement corpus [2], and found similar results.

4.1   Is it Worth Using IE?

The experiments show that the contribution of the IES can be quite high. Reliable annotation can be obtained with limited training, especially when adopting high precision IES configurations. In the case of the CMU corpus, our experiments show that it is possible to move from bootstrapping to active annotation after annotating some dozens of texts. In table 1 we show the amount of training needed for moving to active annotation for each type of information, given a minimum user requirement of 75% precision. This shows that the IES contribution heavily reduces the burden of manual annotation and that such reduction is particularly relevant and immediate in case of quite regular information (e.g., time expressions). In user terms this means that it is possible to focus the activity on annotating more complex pieces of information (e.g. speaker), avoiding to be bothered with repetitive ones (such as stime). With some more training cases the IES is also able to contribute in annotating the complex cases.

Table 1. The amount of training texts needed for reaching at least 75% precision and 50% recall

Tag	Amount of Texts needed for training	Prec	Rec
stime	30	91	78
etime	20	96	72
location	30	82	61
speaker	75	90	50

4.2   Open Issues

A number of issues arise from the experiments. First and foremost our experience shows that the order in which documents are presented to the learner is important. Figure 5 shows the effect of selecting different document sets

---

[2] Where the proposed and correct annotations partially overlap. They count as half correct in calculating precision and recall.

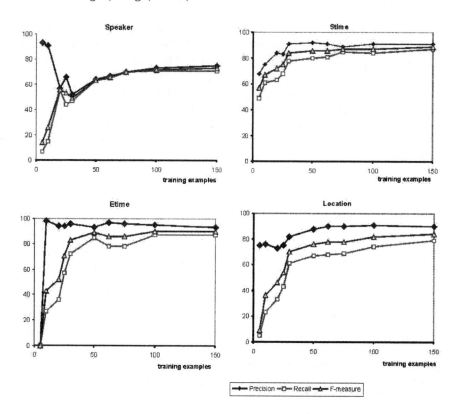

Fig. 4. Bootstrapping where the IES (Amilcare) learns in the background

for training on location. When the IES is presented with a random order its ability to converge to optimal results is limited, probably because of the presence of very similar texts. In this case the learner is not provided with a sufficient variety of cases and therefore it needs more examples to converge. On the contrary by providing the learner with a corpus of documents that are likely to provide new information (we applied the measure of dissimilarity mentioned above to select the next document), the informativity of the training corpus is much bigger and it allows a better convergence of the learner towards an optimal status. For example the random order brings to R=59 and P=82 with 50 documents, while the similarity-based selection provides R=62, P=82 with only 30 texts. This means that users receive a much bigger help using a non-random order of document for training. This is consistent with the Active Learning theory [16], and will require more investigation in the future for a better selection of the training corpus.

A further aspect to be investigated concerns the effect on the user of excellent IES performances after a small amount of annotation. For example when P=97, R=72 is reached after only 30 texts (as in etime), users could

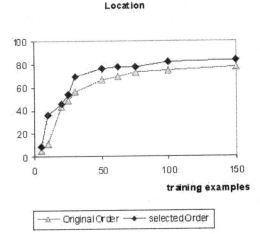

Fig. 5. Comparison of using a random selection of documents for training vs. a similarity-based selection (F-measure)

be tempted to rely on the IES suggestions only, avoiding any further action apart from correction. This would be bad not only for the quality of document annotation, but also for the IES effectiveness. As a matter of fact, each new annotated document is used for further training. Rules are developed using existing annotations. They are tested on the whole corpus to check against false positives (e.g. the rest of the corpus is considered a set of negative examples). A corpus with a relevant number of missing annotations provides a relevant number of (false) negative examples that disorients the leaner, degrading its effectiveness and therefore producing worse future annotation. The entire dimension of the problem is still to be analysed. We are currently considering applying strategies such as randomly removing annotations in order to test the user attention.

5   Conclusion

We have presented a methodology for the interaction between user, interface and IES for human-centred document annotation that both maximizes timeliness and minimizes intrusiveness of the IES suggestions. We have shown experimentally that the effectiveness of the IES in providing annotation is quite high. We are currently applying the resulting system (Melita+Amilcare) for KM and for the SW.

Future work will concern the evaluation of user factors in using IE-based annotation interfaces. Considering that the border between positive proactivity and intrusivity is very thin and subjective, we will perform tests with real users to evaluate the effect of different situations and settings. Moreover we believe that it is important to empower users to maximally customise the degree of proactivity so to obtain the desired behaviour from the IES. The current hardwired mapping between IES settings and user settings is just a partially satisfying solution and we expect to further investigate the issue in the near future.

References

1. Basili, R., Ciravegna, F., Gaizauskas, R. (eds.) (2000) ECAI2000 Workshop on Machine Learning for IE. Berlin. http://www.dcs.shef.ac.uk/~fabio/ecai-workshop.html
2. Califf, M. E. (1998) Relational Learning Techniques for Natural Language IE. Ph.D. thesis. Univ. Texas, Austin. http://www.cs.utexas.edu/users/mecaliff
3. Califf, M. E., Freitag, D., Kushmerick, N., Muslea, I. (eds.) (1999) AAAI-99 Workshop on Machine Learning for Information Extraction. Orlando, Florida. http://www.isi.edu/~muslea/RISE/ML4IE/
4. Cardie, C. Mooney, R. (1999) Special issue on Machine Learning and Natural Language Machine Learning, 11(1-3), 1–5.
5. Ciravegna, F., Kushmenrick, N., Mooney, R. Muslea, I. (eds.) (2001) IJCAI-2001 Workshop on Adaptive Text Extraction and Mining. Held in conjunction with the 17th International Conference on Artificial Intelligence (IJCAI-01), Seattle. http://www.smi.ucd.ie/ATEM2001/
6. Ciravegna, F. (2001) Challenges in Information Extraction from Text for Knowledge Management. IEEE Intelligent Systems 16(6) 88–90.
7. Ciravegna, F. (2001) Adaptive Information Extraction from Text by Rule Induction and Generalisation. In Proc. of 17th International Joint Conference on Artificial Intelligence (IJCAI), Seattle.
8. Ciravegna, F. (2001) (LP)^2, an Adaptive Algorithm for Information Extraction from Web-related Texts. In Proc. of the IJCAI-2001 Workshop on Adaptive Text Extraction and Mining, Seattle.
9. Cunningham, H., Maynard, D., Tablan, V., Ursu, C., Bontcheva, K. (2001) Developing Language Processing Components with GATE. www.gate.ac.uk
10. Day, D., Aberdeen, J., Hirschman, L., Kozierok, R., Robinson, P. Vilain, M. (1997) Mixed-initiative development of language processing systems. In Proc. of the Fifth Conference on Applied Natural Language Processing, Washington.
11. Domingue, J. B., Lanzoni, M., Motta, E., Vargas-Vera, M., Ciravegna, F. (2002) MnM: Ontology driven semi-automatic or automatic support for semantic markup. In Proc. of the 13th International Conference on Knowledge Engineering and Knowledge Management, EKAW02, Siguenza, Spain, Springer Verlag.
12. Freitag, D. (1998) Information Extraction from HTML: Application of a general learning approach. In Proc. of the 15th National Conference on Artificial Intelligence (AAAI-98).
13. Freitag, D., Kushmerick, N. (2000) Boosted wrapper induction. In R. Basili, F. Ciravegna, R. Gaizauskas (eds.) ECAI2000 Workshop on Machine Learning for Information Extraction, Berlin. http://www.dcs.shef.ac.uk/~fabio/ecai-workshop.html

14. Handschuh, S., Staab, S., Ciravegna F. (2002) S-CREAM - Semi-automatic CREAtion of Metadata. In Proc. of the 13th International Conference on Knowledge Engineering and Knowledge Management, EKAW02, Siguenza, Spain, Springer Verlag.
15. Roth, D., Yih, W. (2001) Relational Learning via Propositional Algorithms: An Information Extraction Case Study. In Proc. of 17th International Joint Conference on Artificial Intelligence (IJCAI), Seattle.
16. Thompson, C. A., Califf, M. E. Mooney, R. J. (1999) Active Learning for Natural Language Parsing and Information Extraction. In Proc. of the Sixteenth International Machine Learning Conference (ICML-99), Bled, Slovenia.

Index

3048

Druck und Bindung: Strauss Offsetdruck GmbH